EARLY CHILDHOOD EDUCATION SERIES

Sharon Ryan, *Editor*

ADVISORY BOARD: *Celia Genishi, Doris Fromberg, Carrie Lobman, Rachel Theilheimer, Dominic Gullo, Amita Gupta, Beatrice Fennimore, Sue Grieshaber, Jackie Marsh, Mindy Blaise, Gail Yuen, Alice Honig, Betty Jones, Stephanie Feeney, Stacie G. Goffin, Beth Graue*

Becoming Young Thinkers:
Deep Project Work in the Classroom
JUDY HARRIS HELM

The Early Years Matter: Education, Care, and the Well-Being of Children, Birth to 8
MARILOU HYSON AND HEATHER BIGGAR TOMLINSON

Thinking Critically About Environments for Young Children:
Bridging Theory and Practice
LISA P. KUH, ED.

Standing Up for Something Every Day:
Ethics and Justice in Early Childhood Classrooms
BEATRICE S. FENNIMORE

FirstSchool: Transforming PreK–3rd Grade for African American, Latino,
and Low-Income Children
SHARON RITCHIE & LAURA GUTMANN, EDS.

The States of Child Care: Building a Better System
SARA GABLE

Early Childhood Education for a New Era:
Leading for Our Profession
STACIE G. GOFFIN

Everyday Artists:
Inquiry and Creativity in the Early Childhood Classroom
DANA FRANTZ BENTLEY

Multicultural Teaching in the Early Childhood Classroom:
Approaches, Strategies, and Tools, Preschool–2nd Grade
MARIANA SOUTO-MANNING

Inclusion in the Early Childhood Classroom:
What Makes a Difference?
SUSAN L. RECCHIA & YOON-JOO LEE

Language Building Blocks:
Essential Linguistics for Early Childhood Educators
ANITA PANDEY

Understanding the Language Development and Early Education
of Hispanic Children
EUGENE E. GARCÍA & ERMINDA H. GARCÍA

Moral Classrooms, Moral Children:
Creating a Constructivist Atmosphere in Early Education, 2nd Ed.
RHETA DEVRIES & BETTY ZAN

Defending Childhood:
Keeping the Promise of Early Education
BEVERLY FALK, ED.

Don't Leave the Story in the Book:
Using Literature to Guide Inquiry in Early Childhood Classrooms
MARY HYNES-BERRY

Starting with Their Strengths:
Using the Project Approach in Early Childhood Special Education
DEBORAH C. LICKEY & DENISE J. POWERS

The Play's the Thing:
Teachers' Roles in Children's Play, 2nd Ed.
ELIZABETH JONES & GRETCHEN REYNOLDS

Twelve Best Practices for Early Childhood Education:
Integrating Reggio and Other Inspired Approaches
ANN LEWIN-BENHAM

Big Science for Growing Minds:
Constructivist Classrooms for Young Thinkers
JACQUELINE GRENNON BROOKS

What If All the Kids Are White? Anti-Bias Multicultural Education
with Young Children and Families, 2nd Ed.
LOUISE DERMAN-SPARKS & PATRICIA G. RAMSEY

Seen and Heard:
Children's Rights in Early Childhood Education
ELLEN LYNN HALL & JENNIFER KOFKIN RUDKIN

Young Investigators: The Project Approach in the
Early Years, 2nd Ed.
JUDY HARRIS HELM & LILIAN G. KATZ

Supporting Boys' Learning: Strategies for Teacher Practice, PreK–Grade 3
BARBARA SPRUNG, MERLE FROSCHL, & NANCY GROPPER

Young English Language Learners:
Current Research and Emerging Directions for Practice and Policy
EUGENE E. GARCÍA & ELLEN C. FREDE, EDS.

Connecting Emergent Curriculum and Standards in the Early Childhood Classroom:
Strengthening Content and Teacher Practice
SYDNEY L. SCHWARTZ & SHERRY M. COPELAND

Infants and Toddlers at Work:
Using Reggio-Inspired Materials to Support Brain Development
ANN LEWIN-BENHAM

The View from the Little Chair in the Corner: Improving Teacher Practice and Early
Childhood Learning (Wisdom from an Experienced Classroom Observer)
CINDY RZASA BESS

Culture and Child Development in Early Childhood Programs:
Practices for Quality Education and Care
CAROLLEE HOWES

The Early Intervention Guidebook for Families and Professionals:
Partnering for Success
BONNIE KEILTY

The Story in the Picture:
Inquiry and Artmaking with Young Children
CHRISTINE MULCAHEY

Educating and Caring for Very Young Children:
The Infant/Toddler Curriculum, 2nd Ed.
DORIS BERGEN, REBECCA REID, & LOUIS TORELLI

Beginning School:
U.S. Policies in International Perspective
RICHARD M. CLIFFORD & GISELE M. CRAWFORD, EDS.

Emergent Curriculum in the Primary Classroom
CAROL ANNE WIEN, ED.

Enthusiastic and Engaged Learners
MARILOU HYSON

Powerful Children:
Understanding How to Teach and Learn Using the Reggio Approach
ANN LEWIN-BENHAM

The Early Care and Education Teaching Workforce at the Fulcrum:
An Agenda for Reform
SHARON LYNN KAGAN, KRISTIE KAUERZ, & KATE TARRANT

Windows on Learning:
Documenting Young Children's Work, 2nd Ed.
JUDY HARRIS HELM, SALLEE BENEKE, & KATHY STEINHEIMER

Ready or Not:
Leadership Choices in Early Care and Education
STACIE G. GOFFIN & VALORA WASHINGTON

Supervision in Early Childhood Education, 3rd Ed.
JOSEPH J. CARUSO WITH M. TEMPLE FAWCETT

(continued)

To look for other titles in this series, visit www.tcpress.com

Becoming Young Thinkers

Deep Project Work in the Classroom

Judy Harris Helm

Foreword by Lilian G. Katz

TEACHERS COLLEGE PRESS

TEACHERS COLLEGE | COLUMBIA UNIVERSITY

NEW YORK AND LONDON

naeyc

National Association for the
Education of Young Children
Washington, DC

Published simultaneously by Teachers College Press, 1234 Amsterdam Avenue, New York, NY 10027, and the National Association for the Education of Young Children (NAEYC), 1313 L Street NW, Suite 500, Washington, DC 20005.

Library of Congress Cataloging-in-Publication Data

Helm, Judy Harris.
  Becoming young thinkers : deep project work in the classroom / Judy Harris Helm ; foreword by Lilian G. Katz.
      pages cm
  Includes bibliographical references and index.
  ISBN 978-0-8077-5594-5 (pbk. : alk. paper) —
  ISBN 978-0-8077-7335-2 (ebook)
    1. Project method in teaching—United States. I. Title.
  LB1027.43.H45 2015
  371.3'6—dc23   2014029708

ISBN 978-0-8077-5594-5 (paper)
ISBN 978-0-8077-7335-2 (ebook)

NAEYC Item # 7228

Printed on acid-free paper
Manufactured in the United States of America

22 21 20 19 18 17 16   8 7 6 5 4 3 2

Contents

Foreword

The integration of the project approach into preschool and elementary school curricula has become much more widespread over the past 2 decades. While this comprehensive book informs us of its more than 100-year history, it also provides us with detailed explanations and illustrations of how it can be implemented in the curriculum for a wide age span.

The content is based on Judy Helm's extensive experience of training teachers across the United States, as well as in other countries, on how to launch project work in their classes. The book is rich with detailed examples of how in-depth project work can engage young children and, in the process of doing so, support the vital growth of their minds. Current research on neurological development indicates that the building of a solid foundation of the mind must be well under way by about the first 6 years of life, and it is clear throughout this book how the project approach can have a powerful role in those building processes.

In Part I this book provides teachers with a solid knowledge base of how our predecessors contributed to our understandings of good teaching. Helm incorporates the insights and research of John Dewey and Lev Vygotsky, as well as more recent developmental specialists such as Jerome Bruner, Clancy Blair, and Howard Gardner. All of these discussions can help readers appreciate the long history of educators' efforts to address children's intellects early and to postpone emphasis on academic instruction until children are more ready for it during the early elementary school years. As we can see from the examples Helm shares with us, young children who are fully engaged in deep projects often ask their teachers to help them apply basic academic skills in the service of their intellectual pursuits.

The examples of projects shared throughout the book also show clearly how common it is for parents, teachers, and others with opinions about early education to underestimate young children's intellectual capacities—that is, their capacities to observe events and objects around them and to offer predictions about what might happen following certain events or what might be seen during a field site visit. In addition, it is clear that under the right conditions, children's willingness and abilities to ask questions and to predict (i.e., hypothesize) what the answers to their questions might be seems to be inborn in all youngsters (Katz, 2012). Helm shows us that these important intellectual abilities become stronger in the context of deep project work and, indeed, can lay the foundation for a lifelong disposition to ask questions, seek answers, and make sense of significant events around them. Furthermore, Helm's examples make clear the way in which such deep projects also provide contexts for the development, application, and strengthening of vital social competencies that also have lifelong use and value.

It is important to note also that Helm emphasizes the concept of "deep" project work. Throughout the book, the examples and suggestions she provides make clear the important distinctions between the deep investigations involved in project work versus the fairly common superficial theme activities too often seen in preschool and elementary school classes.

Part II of the book provides detailed examples of strategies for teachers for the in-depth implementation of the project approach. It includes a helpful description of how the webbing of topics helps in the planning and progress of a project. In addition, rich examples of the work of various age groups are described, and the photographs help make clear the practical suggestions that are offered.

Helm also addresses the understandably current preoccupation of teachers with how to address and incorporate the Common Core State Standards. The discussion offers many helpful examples of ways to connect elements of project work to the standards imposed upon teachers of many age levels of children in many educational settings.

In sum, this work brings us up to date with an important and useful component of education—the project approach—that has a history of more than a century in our country and that deserves to be given serious inclusion in the preschool and elementary school curriculum today.

—Lilian G. Katz

REFERENCE

Katz, L. G. (2012). Distinctions between academic versus intellectual goals for young children. *NYSAEC Reporter, 39*(2), 1–15.

Getting to Deep Project Work

This is a book about project work. It is about projects that light up classrooms with child learning, motivate children to make sense of reading and math, and bind children, teachers, and helpful adults into learning communities. It is about children experiencing the joy of solving a problem, investigating a process, and developing confidence in their own ability to learn. It is also about children building mind and brain capacity for successful school experiences, mastering content, and developing self-regulation. Project work can do all this. I have seen it happen in schools across the United States and in other countries.

However, projects do not necessarily result in rich, meaningful learning experiences for children. Projects, like any other learning experience, can vary greatly in quality. Many teachers are confused about what project work is and is not. In an approach to curriculum called the "project approach," the term *project* has a precise meaning. In *Engaging Children's Minds*, Lilian Katz and Sylvia Chard (1989, 2000) define a project in the following way:

> We use the term project to refer to an in-depth study of a particular topic usually undertaken by the whole class working on subtopics in small groups, sometimes by a small group of children within a class, and occasionally by an individual child. The key feature of a project is that it is an investigation—a piece of research that involves children in seeking answers to questions they have formulated themselves or in cooperation with their teacher and that arise as their investigation proceeds. (p. 2)

Even when teachers have a clear understanding of what constitutes project work, they may struggle with how to integrate required curriculum goals with project work. Meeting standards, such as the Common Core State Standards (CCSS; National Governors Association Center for Best Practices & Council of Chief State School Officers, 2010), and providing required experiences from mandated curriculum guides provide additional challenges. Learning how to guide projects is a journey, often a long journey. It is easy to learn the phases or structure of the project approach, how to record what children know in using a web, and how children can represent their learning. It is not so easy for teachers to learn how to help children narrow a topic to a meaningful investigation, how to guide children to create their own representations without taking over, or what to do to provoke higher-level thinking. I have noticed that teachers whom I see doing deep, meaningful project work will sometimes say they are "working on how to do project work," "getting better at guiding projects," or "starting to get the hang of it!" There is a lot to learn about project work. Like their children, project teachers are eager learners and deep thinkers.

Teachers of young children who are not familiar with the project approach should begin their journey with the book *Young Investigators: The Project Approach in the Early Years* (Helm & Katz, 2011). For teachers who have some experience with projects and want to deepen their project work, I have written this book for you.

WHAT DO HIGH-QUALITY DEEP PROJECTS LOOK LIKE?

A vision of deep project work is contained in some of the definitions associated with *deep* and *deepen*: profound; intellectual depth and insight; intensity of feeling or quality. Deep projects, when they occur in classrooms, have characteristics that enable the children to experience intellectual insight and depth of thinking. Deep project work is strongly connected to the children's world, involving them emotionally and sustaining intense interest. The deep project is sensory-rich with authentic artifacts and integration of complex knowledge. Deep projects provoke children to think deeply, to analyze, to synthesize new ideas and create meaningful artistic expressions, constructions, and other creations. In deep project work, teachers are colearners. Deep projects motivate children to learn and practice academic skills, and support curriculum goals and achievement of standards. Often deep projects involve children in authentic explorations of the work that adults do.

HOW TO GET THERE: AN OVERVIEW OF THIS BOOK

In any journey it is helpful to have a clear image of where one wants to go and a map of routes to follow. A teacher who wants her classroom to be alive with deep project work will benefit from developing an understanding of the foundations of the project approach as explained in Part I of this book. Chapter 1 connects new knowledge about the mind and brain with project work and provides a list of instructional guidelines for all learning experiences. Chapter 2 focuses on insights from psychology and pedagogy on the foundations of the project approach and defines deep project work. The chapters in Part II take up the implementation of deep project work and provide specific strategies and methods. These include selecting topics, planning, questioning by children, questioning by teachers, representing ideas, and creating provocations to promote engagement and deep thinking. The appendixes provide specific information and worksheets that will be helpful for teachers undertaking deep projects.

A PERSONAL JOURNEY

This book is also about my own personal journey, or to be more accurate, about many, many journeys. It is about what I have learned over the past 20 years consulting and training teachers of young children about how to do project work, how to document, and how to share the wonderful experiences occurring in their classrooms. It is about real teachers in real classrooms from El Paso, Texas, to Quebec, Canada; from Oregon to Massachusetts; and from Scotland to China to Mexico. All of these teachers, directors, and principals were on their own journeys of learning how to teach and how to light a fire for learning in the hearts of those children whose care and education were entrusted to them for a very short period of time. I learned from these teachers. As I go from program to program, school to school, teacher to teacher, I take what I learned from one teacher and share it with another. I take what a teacher discovered worked for her and propose it as a possibility to another teacher who is struggling with the same challenge thousands of miles away. I lift up good teaching and exciting triumphs and share them through my speeches, trainings, articles, and books.

One training program that is committed to project work, the Early Childhood Connections Program, is sponsored by the Kohl Children's Museum of Greater Chicago. Since 2001 we have trained over 1,000 teachers and providers in child-care centers and schools in the Chicago Public Schools. Over 31,000 children and their families have been introduced to project work. By gathering pre- and post-implementation data, we have fine-tuned the training process and identified many of the stumbling blocks that teachers encounter in learning to do project work. Data gathering included a 17-item Likert-type observation instrument based on the Early Childhood Environment Rating Scale (ECERS) (Harms, Clifford, & Cryer, 1998) to determine the participants' ability to align goals and standards set by the National Association for the Education of Young Children (NAEYC), Illinois State Board of Education, and Chicago Public Schools with the project approach.

This instrument has been used for the Early Childhood Connections project since 2002. During the years between 2001 and 2006 a pretest–posttest quasi-experimental group design with 186 participating teachers compared intervention and control groups in matched pairs. These teachers were matched according to grade levels taught and populations served. Comparisons between pretests and posttests and between intervention and control groups indicated that the Early Childhood Connections Program produced statistically significant and practically meaningful positive changes in teacher attitudes toward the project-based approach and an increase in the use of developmentally appropriate methods and strategies by early childhood teachers in their classrooms (Perney, 2006). Ongoing observations in classrooms and pre- and post-surveys helped us fine-tune the training process and identified many of the stumbling blocks that teachers encountered in learning to do project work. In 2007 the museum extended the program to reach family child-care providers and child-care centers. The museum continues to evaluate a small sample group each year and is completing year 3 of field testing of a fidelity scale that will enable the measurement of the level of implementation of the project approach.

To make sure that this book and the second-level training incorporated what teachers truly wanted to know and what was missing in their project teaching, a survey of experienced project teachers was created (Helm, 2011). The online Deepening Project Work Survey was sent to past participants in the Kohl program, to teachers and members of the Illinois Project Group, and other programs across the country where I knew project work was occurring. Over 160 participants completed the survey, with 81% having guided three or more projects. The teachers who completed the survey indicated that they desired help with the following topics: recognizing questions that lead to deep investigations, strengthening intellectual dispositions, facilitating higher-level questioning, adding teacher provocations to project work, and integrating technology into their projects. Over

46% indicated they needed help with standards. Encouragingly, 68% said that they read books about project work; hence the motivation for me to write this book.

I am deeply indebted to my colleagues and friends throughout the country who have provided access to their classrooms, their work, their children's work, and volumes of documentation of exciting projects. Those whose work is in this book include Amber Forrest and Heidi LaBounty of Seeds of Faith Preschool; Michelle Fernandes and Lora Taylor of Northminster Learning Center; Barbara Gallick of Illinois State University Child Care Center; Dana Gorman of Community Cooperative Nursery School in Rowayton, Connecticut; Dawn Johnson of Kids' World Day Care and Preschool in Centerville, Iowa; Christine Davidson, Maryanne Gallagher, and Maryanne Baskin of the Center for Early Education and Care at the University of Massachusetts; Nick Pettit, 2nd-grade teacher at Scuola Vita Nuova Charter School in Kansas City, Missouri; Clarese Ornstein at the Early Education Center, Round Lake Community Unit School District 116; Mary Trieschmann, who began the Kohl project; and Erika Miller-Gray, Stephanie Bynum, Sarah Mack, and Patricia Knable of the education department of Kohl Children's Museum. The staff of UPC Discovery in Peoria, Illinois, provided not only access to their wonderful project work but also thoughtful reviews of each chapter of the book. These include Pam Scranton, Karen Coyle, Katrina Larson, Susan Bandolino, Stephanie Randall, Malerie Byrne, and Mary Ann Gottlieb. I have been blessed in all my books to have Susan Liddicoat of Teachers College Press as my content editor. She has not only provided an amazing attention to detail but also, through her questions, has challenged me to clarify my thinking. This book could not have been written without Tracey Tokuhama-Espinosa's gracious sharing of her inspiring work on mind, brain, and education science; and Lilian Katz, who reviewed the manuscript and has provided insight, inspiration, and support throughout my career.

Now let's begin the journey anew.

Part I

FOUNDATIONS OF THE PROJECT APPROACH

CHAPTER 1

Connecting New Knowledge About the Brain with the Project Approach

Michelle Fernandes's classroom of 3- and 4-year-old children is a very busy place. Children are intensely focused on a variety of activities. The interest of most of the children on this morning appears to be the Seed Store Project. On a bulletin board by the door is a word wall where words such as *kernel, seed coat,* and *germinate* are illustrated with children's drawings. The housekeeping corner has been transformed by the children into a seed store using hollow blocks from the block area for seed bins and a variety of equipment and signs, obviously child-made. A large machine created and used by the children mixes and dispenses seeds into sales bags. Some children are using watercolor paint at an art table. Although they can paint whatever they wish, most of the paintings are related to flowers, seeds, and plants. Seedlings in clear plastic cups fill the windowsills. The book corner has books about seeds, flowers, and planting, along with books about nature and flower photographs. On an easel chart in the center of the room is a web created that morning in circle time, as the children dictated their thoughts about what they now know about seeds. As the seed store did a brisk business in selling seeds, children moved in and out of the various activities.

One table, however, appeared to hold the attention of a small group of children. For about 45 minutes these 3- and 4-year-old children investigated the process of weighing seeds with a round scale. The children were intrigued by the scale and the different kinds of seeds. A few children came over to investigate it. One child, Nolan, started pouring sunflower seeds onto the scale. Michelle asked if he noticed the red pointer on the scale and

if anything happened to it when he poured the seeds on the scale. The children noticed the pointer and saw that it was moving. Michelle said, "I wonder how it is moving?" "I wonder if you could make the pointer move all the way over to here," she said while pointing to the end point of the scale. This provocation created much discussion, theorizing, and experimentation. Nolan thought that maybe if they tipped the scale on its side, the pointer would move (see Figure 1.1). The children tried that. It didn't move. Then they thought that it might move if they all just walked away and left it alone for awhile. Michelle suggested making a mark where the pointer was with a marker so they would know if it moved when they came back. They marked the scale and then all the children left the table for a few minutes until Nolan, who appeared to be leading the investigation, said it was time to come back. When the children returned to the table, they discovered that the pointer had not moved.

Michelle then summarized their work and challenged them by saying, "Turning it on its side didn't work, and walking away didn't work. I wonder what else you could try." They then tried placing corn kernels on the scale, replacing the sunflower seeds. This made the pointer move from the marked area and created great excitement. The teacher then encouraged them to try all the different kinds of seeds they had to see what would happen to the pointer. They noticed how the pointer moved along the window with different seeds. Another child then had the idea to start adding seeds together to make the pointer move more. After they experimented for awhile, Michelle asked them, "So why does the pointer move with different seeds?" Nolan then said that he thought the bigger seeds made the pointer move more. Michelle asked them to hold a cup of each kind of seed filled to approximately the same height in each hand and compare. They were able to tell that some cups were heavier even though the seeds themselves were smaller. When Michelle questioned the children further, they concluded it probably wasn't the size of the individual seed but how heavy the seeds were. The corn kernels were heavier than the sunflower seeds, and the scale measures how heavy things are. Satisfied with their conclusions, they left the table to do other interesting things. Pushing back his chair from the table, Nolan said, "Mrs. Fernandes, I'm tired; that was hard work!"

THE PROJECT APPROACH IN ACTION: ENGAGED MEANINGFUL LEARNING

The description of Michelle's classroom during the Seed Store Project is typical of a preschool classroom filled with rich, thought-provoking project work. The room has a wealth of materials and artifacts; children are engaged in hands-on experiences; and children represent what they have learned in a variety of ways. Displays and documentation provide evidence that the children have interacted with adults who work with seeds (see Figures 1.2–1.5).

Typical of classrooms using the project approach, not every child is participating in the project at the same time or doing the same type of work. Children are also involved in other learning experiences unrelated to the project topic: Some children are painting at the easel, some are listening to stories at a listening center, and others are completing puzzles. Project work continues side by side with other developmentally appropriate activities. Yet consistently most of the children come back in some way or another that morning to their interest in seeds and, more specifically, the seed store. Not only are they interested in learning about the topic, they also are so invested in it that they create their own play environment (the seed store) and sustain play within it for days. The children continue to focus drawings, paintings, and experimentation on the topic for weeks.

Figure 1.1. Nolan tests his theory that placing the scale on its side will make the pointer move.

Watching Michelle's classroom, visitors comment that the children appear very focused and purposeful in their work. Children are thoroughly involved in what they are doing and move from area to area of the room without direction. Although one might expect that this is a noisy classroom, visitors also marvel that Michelle's classroom appears so quiet. More than likely one of the reasons for the quiet is that children are thinking. They have something to think about that is very interesting to them. This is a classroom where children are engaged, and the teacher knows how to foster engagement in children.

The focus of this book is how to create and sustain classrooms, just like Michelle's, where active, engaging, thought-provoking learning experiences occur. Many teachers, reading about Michelle's classroom, might be thinking that these activities and learning experiences are familiar to them. Most early childhood teachers at some time in their career have had plants sprouting on their windowsill,

Figure 1.2. Children observe the seed-mixing machine on their visit to a seed store.

Figure 1.3. Children decide that the large hollow blocks might be a good way to begin making their own seed store.

Figure 1.4. The children create a hole in their machine to put the seeds in to be mixed.

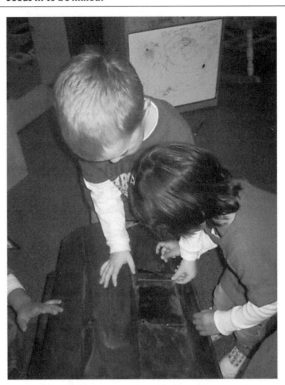

Figure 1.5. The finished mixing machine is painted red to match the one they saw in the seed store.

children painting flowers, and books about plants in their reading corner. However, this exploration of the seed store is, in fact, a child-driven investigation, a project led by the children. Michelle has followed the structure of the project approach, which means that it is an investigation directed by children's questions and curiosity and that the children own that investigation. This is evident from the web that includes questions children asked, the representations they made, the interaction with adult experts, and most of all, the intense engagement of the children. This engagement is what motivates a child like Nolan and his 3- and 4-year-old friends to spend 45 minutes trying to solve one problem, to think very hard, and to persist until they figure out the answer. No one needed to tell Nolan that he was doing good work or a good job. He realized himself that he and his classmates had worked hard and accomplished something. Teachers often ask how they can teach this way—specifically, how to not just do project work, but also to create rich, deep, meaningful investigations that not only engage children but also accomplish curriculum goals and meet standards such as the Common Core State Standards. Teachers want to build children's intellectual capacity and dispositions for lifelong learning.

SCIENTIFICALLY SUBSTANTIATED ART OF TEACHING

There is much discussion and debate today about what students need to prepare them for the 21st century (Gardner, 1999; Rotherham & Willingham, 2009). Gardner (2008) cautions that we need to think globally about this issue, as our children will be citizens of a fast-paced, ever-changing world. When young children who are currently in preschool and early elementary school become adults, they will have challenges and opportunities that we can't possibly anticipate. In addition to important literacy and numeracy skills, they will have to be good problem solvers, flexible thinkers, and eager learners as they encounter a rapidly changing technology, the global job market, and the environmental challenges of a growing world population.

There is a significant impetus to reform education in response to these anticipated changes. This has resulted in more closely monitoring what children are learning, including elaborate assessment and benchmarking, to be sure that children develop academic skills. This effort comes from many directions, with one of the most prominent, the Common Core State Standards (CCSS), coming from the National Governors Association Center for Best Practices and the Council of Chief State School Officers (2010). The CCSS are voluntary standards adopted by states. The purpose of the standards is to establish clear, consistent guidelines for what every student should know and be able to do in math and English language arts from kindergarten through 12th grade. Some researchers fear that this has resulted in a narrowed curriculum that focuses only on easily measured academic skills (Au, 2007; Jennings & Rentner, 2006; Morton & Dalton, 2007). However, the CCSS can be helpful in guiding teachers as to what curriculum content they should be integrating into project work.

21st-Century Learning

Although academic skills are still a key to success, they are unlikely to be sufficient in the rapidly changing world of the 21st century. In addition, children need to develop brain and mind capacity to be continual and enthusiastic learners, to be independent and self-directed with problem-solving skills, and to become adults with an intense desire to figure things out, think creatively, and be persistent and collaborative. According to Gardner (2008), they will need disciplined, synthesizing, creating, respectful, and ethical minds. Rich learning experiences such as those seen in the Seed Store Project (see Figures 1.6 and 1.7) can integrate knowledge and skills and enable children to not only learn the value of these skills but also provide opportunities to practice them. In highly engaging investigations, academics can become meaningful and exciting and at the same time place a child on a trajectory for developing an inquiring mind, a commitment to lifelong learning, and an intellectually fulfilling life. It is not that academics aren't important, but that it will take more than academics to prepare children for the future. According to Rotherham & Willingham (2009),

> The debate is not about content versus skills. There is no responsible constituency arguing against ensuring that students learn how to think in school. Rather, the issue is how to meet the challenges of delivering content and skills in a rich way that genuinely improves outcomes for students. (p. 16)

As an early childhood teacher, teacher educator, administrator, and finally consultant, I have spent my professional life learning how to make this kind of classroom a reality for more children. Unfortunately, Michelle's classroom is not typical of educational experiences for our youngest students. Some children are in prekindergarten through 2nd-grade classrooms that, at best, could be described as inappropriate for their developmental age and lacking in stimulation. Some of the classrooms, at worst, can be characterized as deserts of intellectual thought, uninspiring, and ineffective as preparation for school success and learning the skills needed for

Figure 1.7. As children view descriptions of seeds and their prices, they learn how being able to read, write, and use numbers is important for them.

the 21st century. I have come to think about providing experiences like the Seed Store Project to all children as an equity issue. Children who have difficulty in school and who face challenges of poverty, learning a second language, or coping with special needs appear to also be in early environments that are increasingly oriented toward early academics, rote learning, and emphasis on drill and practice. The result is that children who would benefit the most from rich and engaging prekindergarten, kindergarten, and primary learning experiences instead are placed in the most didactic classrooms. Some prominent proponents of 21st-century skills such as the George Lucas Foundation, founding body of Edutopia.org, have advocated that project work become a core strategy for preparing children for the 21st century. To make that happen, educators need to update their beliefs and understandings of how children actually learn.

Beginning with the Brain

Technology has changed our understanding of how the brain learns and how we develop intellect by enabling us to "see" through the skull and observe the brain in action. Until this happened, what occurred in a child's head was theory and speculation based on what children do and say. If a child could not count, then later could count, we concluded that something had happened within the head of that child to create this change. Educational theory and much of the advice on how to teach children

Figure 1.6. When interacting with adults who share their interest, children learn how to have meaningful conversations and get answers to questions.

were based on observation and then speculation. No one really knew what happened in the brain.

Near the end of the 20th century, we began to get glimpses of how learning occurs through technology such as scans and sophisticated monitoring equipment that could also capture changes in heart rate, breathing, and even the rate of sucking of babies using a pacifier. In the early 1970s CAT (computerized axial tomography) scans, later also called CT scans, enabled a more accurate viewing of the structures of the brain. In the 1980s MRI (magnetic resonance imaging) provided high-quality two- and three-dimensional images of the brain. In the 1990s fMRI (functional magnetic resonance imaging) captured blood flow in the brain, and we were at last able to see what neural activity looked like.

As neuroimaging became more and more sophisticated, those who studied the process of learning eagerly jumped on findings from neuroscience, applying these directly to teaching. Unfortunately, some of these applications turned out to be "bridges too far" and in the end were found not to be scientifically sound (Tokuhama-Espinosa, 2010). I list here some of these misunderstandings (in italic), followed by what we now know:

- *Listening to Mozart makes you smarter.* Improvement of test scores is only short term.
- *The brain is like a computer with limited memory storage.* The brain grows the more it is used; and the more it knows (the more neural connections made), the greater the capacity to learn more.
- *It's all over by age 3.* The brain is actually "plastic," meaning it changes its own wiring (Zull, 2011) and is able to develop new connections. Critical (or nonreversible) periods are not applicable to cognitive thinking. There are periods, called sensitive periods, when it is somewhat easier for children to learn some things, but the difference is probably overrated.
- *People are either "left-brained" or "right-brained."* The idea that each hemisphere of the brain learns differently and that teachers have neglected the "right side" is

not grounded in neuroscience. All complex cognitive processes are integrated and use extensive networks.

The hoopla over these "insights" and the discrediting that followed left educators wary. Drawing valid implications for classroom practice from the work of neuroscientists was difficult for educators. It was also difficult for neuroscientists to comprehend the world of teaching and suggest valid applications. There is, however, enormous potential in using the research and drawing truly valid implications for educational practice, and the first glimmers of educational neuroscientific research are promising (Fischer & Immordino-Yang, 2008). When there are many children struggling in school and leaving school without the skills to be successful, it would be sad if educators ignored what neuroscientists are learning that might help some children. Neuroscientists also have found it frustrating that their research is not reaching educators.

> Coherent translation of cognitive neuroscience to education is sparse. We need to translate knowledge about how children learn in ways that are relevant to teachers' work in school settings. Educational policymakers and administrators focus on the external structures of education, such as standards, data analysis, scheduling, curriculum, school governance and accountability, yet they pay little attention to the learners themselves. (Hardiman & Denckla, 2010, "Obstacles to Uniting Science and Education," para. 2)

Mind, Brain, and Education Science

It is one thing to avoid taking a bridge too far, but the solution is not to give up building bridges. Since 2000, there has been a growing movement to re-create those bridges, to conceptualize a scientifically substantiated art of teaching, perhaps a biologically based revolution (Fischer & Immordino-Yang, 2008). A number of researchers from biology, education, and the cognitive and developmental sciences have begun to collaborate.

It might be helpful here to provide some clarification of terminology as we begin to examine the results of this collaboration:

- The *brain* is the portion of the nervous system enclosed in the skull that coordinates sensory input, motor responses, and the process of learning.
- *Neuroscience* is the branch of life sciences that deals with the physiology of learning, the brain, the nervous system, and how these relate to behavior and learning.
- The term *mind* is generally used to describe conscious mental events such as feeling, perceiving, thinking, will, and, especially, reason.
- *Education* is imparting or acquiring general knowledge and skills, developing powers of reasoning and judgment, and preparing oneself or others intellectually for mature life (Education, n.d.).

All of these have been studied as separate sciences (neuroscience, psychology, pedagogy) and in various combinations, such as educational neuroscience.

In 2004 the International Mind, Brain and Education Society was formed to effectively bridge the gaps between these sciences (Dawson & Fischer, 1994; Fischer, 2009; Fischer et al., 2007). Their goal is to develop resources for scientists, practitioners, public policymakers, and the public; and create and identify useful information, research directions, and promising educational practices. In 2008 Tokuhama-Espinosa (2008, 2010) facilitated a study to define standards for this new collaborative science of Mind, Brain, and Education and to separate myths from the facts. This effort supported interaction and joint reflection by bringing together experts in these fields to address and reach a consensus regarding the applicability of neuroscience research to teaching and learning. The study utilized grounded-theory development to determine the parameters of this new field with a meta-analysis of over 2,200 documents from the past 30 years. This was followed by a Delphi survey (a survey process for a group to reach agreement) of 20 international experts from six different countries that further refined the science content over several months of reflection. These findings were further reviewed by 8 more experts. Finally the revised model was compared to existing information sources, including the popular press, peer review journals, academic publications, teacher training textbooks, and the Internet. The outcome resulted in standards for the emerging new field, now labeled Mind, Brain and Education (also called MBE Science).

Additionally, the Delphi expert panel focused on the goals of the new discipline, its history, the thought leaders, and a model for judging the quality of information. The study culminated in a model of a new academic discipline of Mind, Brain, and Education Science, with 12 tenets that address individual learning, 21 principles of learning that are true for all learners, and 10 instructional guidelines, all supported by the meta-analysis of the literature and the Delphi response (Tokuhama-Espinosa, 2010).

The group classified the information about the brain and learning identified in the literature review into four categories:

- What is well-established
- What is probably so
- What is intelligent speculation
- What is popular misconception or myth

In addition to agreement among the panel of experts, these concepts were also subjected to criteria from *Best Evidence Encyclopedia* and *What Works Clearinghouse*. All of this work is now available for teachers to develop a valid, applicable neuroscience foundation. Those concepts classified by the group as *well established* and *probably so* are applicable for use in teaching and are listed in Appendix A. In the following paragraph, I have taken these concepts and briefly summarized them into a vision of learning for classrooms of young children, prekindergarten through early primary school:

> Each child's mind and brain capacity is unique and is shaped by the child's experiences and the context of those experiences. Children innately search for meaning that provides motivation to learn new things. Children learn best when learning experiences begin with what they already know and capitalize on emotional involvement with the content. When children actively construct their own

knowledge (rather than simply memorize what others have learned), they are more likely to be motivated to engage in the learning experience. The ways in which learning experiences are organized and presented can increase children's memory. Experiences that help children develop self-regulation (monitoring oneself via executive function; see Chapter 2) can aid them in developing higher-order thinking skills.

MBE SCIENCE INSTRUCTIONAL GUIDELINES

From the individual concepts, the group of experts also agreed upon a set of specific instructional guidelines (Tokuhama-Espinosa, 2010, pp. 114–124). These are especially helpful for examining strategies and methods of instruction. These validated guidelines, which apply to all ages, are summarized below and expanded in Figure 1.8.

1. *Learning Environments.* Create environments "with physical and mental security, respect, intellectual freedom, self-regulation, paced challenges, feedback, and active learning." (p. 114)
2. *Sense and Meaning.* "Try to link what is taught in class with applications to the students' lives." (p. 116)
3. *Memory.* "Appreciate the complex nature of memory and understand the vital link between memory and learning." Vary your classroom activities "to take advantage of different memory systems." (p. 117)
4. *Attention Spans.* "Understand that students have limited attention spans, which vary by individual, subject matter, and activity." Avoid "passive activities, which can easily bore students." Opt for the delivery of information using proven methods and strategies that engage learners and maximize opportunities to gain new knowledge. (p. 119)
5. *The Social Nature of Learning.* "Understand that learning often occurs in social contexts, such as classrooms, . . . [and] it can often be enhanced through social interaction."

Structure teaching activities to encourage social exchanges. (pp. 119–120)
6. *The Mind-Body Connection.* Understand the ways that "the body impacts the mind, and the mind controls the body." Build background knowledge about "the ways nutrition, sleep, and exercise impact learning." (p. 120)
7. *Orchestrated Immersion.* Realize that classrooms are "filled with different types of students, with different brain content from different past experiences, and with different preferences for ways to receive new information. . . . Consider these differences to be an opportunity," rather than a problem. "Create interactions that integrate the strengths and weaknesses of learners" in such a way as to maximize the experiences of all. (p. 121)
8. *Active Processes.* "To be engaged, learners need to be involved. Such involvement" is often active (although reflective processes are also important). "Know when and how to integrate active learning experiences" into classroom activities to "enhance learning potential." (p. 122)
9. *Metacognition.* "Time for reflection . . . [and] to 'think about thinking'" elevates "the overall conceptual grasp of new knowledge." "Incorporate activities that stimulate metacognition." (p. 122)
10. *Learning Throughout the Life Span.* Understand that "human brains have a high degree of plasticity and continue to develop throughout the life span. . . . Human learning is achieved through developmental processes, which follow a universal pattern for most skills, including academic skills shared across literate cultures, such as reading, writing, math . . . . There are 'sensitive periods' (*not* critical periods) in human brain development during which certain skills are learned with greater ease than at other times. . . . Take advantage of this [fact] to teach skills at an appropriate time, based on the characteristics of the learner. . . . Understand that there are wider windows for learning than previously thought." (p. 123)

These guidelines, agreed upon by experts from neuroscience, psychology, and education, point the way to education in the future. If project work is a part of your classroom, you have probably already recognized that project work provides learning experiences consistent with these guidelines. In fact, these guidelines provide a structure for examining the validity of the project approach as a method of instruction. The analysis in Figure 1.8 shows how MBE Science instructional guidelines are met in the project approach, consistent with what is now known about the science of teaching and learning. As we study the process of guiding project work in this book, we will revisit these guidelines frequently, as they can provide a framework for increasing the depth and effectiveness of project work.

CHILDREN'S INTELLECTUAL CAPACITY

When I was born in central Illinois in the 1940s, my parents believed that children's intellectual abilities were set at birth. One might have a child who is smart, average, or, well, not so smart. The job of the parent was to accept and love that child no matter the potential. In the schools of my childhood, children were quickly sorted, especially into reading groups where they would receive instruction matched to their potential. In the nature (genes, G) versus nurture (environment, E) debate of that time, nature was winning. As we began to understand how the environment (e.g., interactions, health, and stimulation) can impact children's ability to learn and how an environment could inhibit a child's learning, nature plus nurture (G + E) became the accepted paradigm. Today through research in neuroscience and genetics we are beginning to glimpse a new paradigm (Shenk, 2010), which is based on the understanding that genes do matter but environment can actually shape genes. In the end "each of us is a dynamic system, a creature of development" (p. 20). Genes are in fact shaped by experiences. "We don't *inherit* traits from our genes, we develop traits through the dynamic process of gene–environment interaction" (p. 21). The environment

can shape the expression of genes and in fact can physically change genes. A more accurate representation of this interactionist model would be G × E (Genes times Environment), "a dynamic process with every input at every level influencing every other input" (p. 29). An organism at birth can develop in a number of different ways, and how that organism develops is determined by what it experiences in its life. This concept applies also to the development of the mind and intellect, to the power of knowing, the ability to understand, and the capacity for rational and intelligent thought. As Shenk (2010) says,

> Intelligence is not an innate aptitude, hardwired at conception or in the womb, but a collection of developing skills driven by the interaction between genes and environment. No one is born with a predetermined amount of intelligence. Intelligence (and IQ scores) can be improved. Few adults come close to their true intellectual potential. (p. 32)

Although most of the science behind this *interactionist* theory became available in the last part of the 20th century, the belief that intelligence is permanently set by genes continues to color our approaches to children and learning. Many teachers and parents, and great-grandparents like my 100-year-old father, can still be heard to say such things as "You got a smart one there!" What we now understand is that thinking about intelligence as a set characteristic was probably wrong. A valid implication from the world of neuroscience is that the brain and the ability to think are shaped by experiences (Zull, 2002). Although there are, of course, some limits on the shaping, on the whole children's intellect, their intelligence, is affected by what they encounter in their environment. The brain is shaped by the way and amount of thinking that it does.

Earlier models of the brain discouraged us from thinking about the changing capacity to learn. "They tended to present the brain as fixed, with the wiring necessary for learning already in place—somewhat like an automobile, a machine that does not change when someone drives it" (Zull, 2004, p. 68).

Figure 1.8. MBE Science Instructional Guidelines and the Project Approach

Instructional Guidelines	Implications for Instruction	How the Instructional Guidelines Occur in Project Work
Instructional Guideline 1: Learning Environments	"Good learning environments are made, not found." Teachers model and require respectful intellectual exchanges. Learning experiences begin with "assessment of what students already know." Teachers have "a clear vision of what students need to know to learn." "Learning activities that are student-centered and dynamic." (p. 115)	Small-group, large-group, and teacher/child conversations occur regularly as a topic is selected; children discuss what they know about the topic and then generate questions for investigation. Teachers plan integration of required curriculum and standards by anticipating child needs in the investigation and opportunities for children to learn and practice academic skills. Children plan how to represent what they learn through drawing, writing, painting, presentations, and building models and play environments.
Instructional Guideline 2: Sense and Meaning	Teachers "link what is taught in class with applications to the students' lives." Teachers know students' needs. "Facts and skills are embedded in authentic experiences (natural contexts)." Teachers appreciate students' "culturally based neural network (knowledge)." (p. 116)	Project topics are chosen based on relevance to children's lives and child interest. During anticipatory planning the teacher identifies where learning knowledge and skills *naturally occur* in the topic. For example, in a project on shoes the teacher anticipates that numeral recognition will naturally occur as children study shoe sizes and prices. The teacher uses the children's interest and involvement in shoes to assess numeral knowledge and teach numerals.

Instructional Guideline 3: Memory	Teachers "understand the vital link between memory and learning."
	
	"Modes of instruction take advantage of different sensory pathways in the brain."
	
	Teachers "teach to auditory, visual, and kinesthetic pathways . . . to improve the chances of recall."
	
	Experiences utilize the three forms of long-term memory:
	• Associative memory—"links past knowledge with new information"
	• "Emotionally important or value-laden memory"—"what the student gives importance to"
	• Survival-value memory—"students learn things that help them survive"
	
	Recall experiences help students "develop a 'habit of mind' about how to store and retrieve important information." (p. 117)
		The project process maximizes memory. As children investigate, they
		• make notes, take photographs, draw pictures, create models, design and use play environments, give presentations, organize materials, and so on
		• interview experts in large and small groups, read books, view videos and photos, discuss findings, theories, and ideas for representation of what they learned
		• utilize all three forms of long-term memory by
		  ✓ beginning the project by remembering and sharing what they know about the topic
		  ✓ investigating topics that are relevant and of high emotional interest
		  ✓ learning and using academic skills because they need them to do their work (e.g., tallying because they want to know how many windows they need in their construction; learning how to ask questions because they want to get answers from experts)
		• discuss their findings, reviewing each day the status of the process and their goals

Instructional Guideline 4: Attention Spans	Attention spans "vary by individual, subject, and activity." Teachers should • "minimize passive activities" • engage learners and maximize opportunities to gain new knowledge • vary experiences with persons (teacher to student, for example), place (a change of seat), or topic at least every 20 minutes Students reflect and summarize new information to maximize memory consolidation. Teachers use primacy-recency principle. Children will "remember best what occurs first, second best what occurs last, and least what occurs in the middle." (pp. 118–119)	Project work is active learning. The project process requires experiences that children find engaging such as visiting field sites, interacting with adults who are experts on the topic, and investigating authentic artifacts. Children review and share their findings with the group on a regular basis, often daily when project work is going on. Teachers document what children are doing with photographs and notes that are shared with children for reflection. Children also take photographs and discuss what they have observed.
Instructional Guideline 5: The Social Nature of Learning	"Learning often occurs in social contexts" and "can often be enhanced through social interaction, as in student group work or discussions." Teaching activities should "encourage active exchanges of perceptions and information." Encouraging debate enables students "to think critically and to interact with each other" and "prepares them to deal with counter opinions." Small-group work "requires a few students to interact collaboratively." Orchestrate activities "in such a way as to encourage maximum participation and thus allow students to construct their own learning." (pp. 119–120)	Project work in the early years of schooling is done in groups of children. Groups of children may focus on a specific aspect of a project such as the wheels of a truck. The teacher and children create webs and lists of what they know and what they have learned, which children review when deciding on next steps in the process. Children create plans for representing what they have learned. They may create models or play environments, plays or presentations. Children discuss what to do and how to do it. Theories and plans are shared, recorded, and revisited by the group.

Instructional Guideline 6: Mind–Body Connection	Teachers teach children about nutrition, sleep, and exercise. Teachers recognize that "students' brains learn best when the needs of the body are met." (p. 120)	Project work often provides opportunities for teachers to integrate knowledge about the needs of their bodies (e.g., topics on health-related facilities such as the dentist's office, food providers such as restaurants, or sports and hobbies). Because project work is centered on topics of great interest to children, knowledge and skills developed during the investigation are easily learned and remembered. Project work in classrooms more often occurs during flexible work times, enabling response to children's individual attention and activity levels.
Instructional Guideline 7: Orchestrated Immersion	Teachers create interactions that integrate the strengths and weaknesses of the learners to maximize experiences of all, "similar to an orchestra director who immerses students in complex experiences that support learning by calling on individuals one by one to bring out their voices and then weaving them into a single class experience." "Teachers integrate different gifts and help each player perform to their best abilities for the good of the group." "This means picking up on all of the cues students provide in class." (p. 121)	Project work involves many different kinds of activities so each child has many opportunities to contribute to the project and to focus on aspects of the topic of the most interest. All children have a place in the project. The role of the teacher is to enable the complex process of project work to occur through classroom management and access to resources and experts. The teacher documents and assesses throughout the project process so that children are learning knowledge and skills appropriate for each child's developmental needs and skill level. The teacher uses anticipatory planning that maps the concepts and skills that can authentically be encountered in the project so opportunities are not missed. Anticipatory planning includes special needs and abilities of all children in the classroom.
Instructional Guideline 8: Active Processes	Teachers must integrate active learning and reflective activities to enhance learning potential. Active learning classrooms include • more than passive listening • opportunities to use higher-order thinking skills • less emphasis on knowledge transmission and greater emphasis on developing skills • encouragement to explore attitudes and values • immediate feedback from teachers (Bonwell & Eison, 1991) Teachers should "design significant learning experiences that require students to act on their own knowledge. This means teachers not only help students acquire knowledge; they also show them how to put that knowledge into action in order to develop skills." (p. 122)	Project work is active learning, even when the children are involved in listening to experts or having reading materials related to the topic read to them. Because they are investigating with specific knowledge goals about the topic, they are involved in actively listening and looking for specific information. Higher-order thinking skills are developed as children generate questions for investigation, analyze data and findings, and hypothesize about what experts might tell them or how a process might work. Children think about what they have learned, talk about it, and plan as a group how to create representations related to what they have learned about the topic. Projects usually involve a significant amount of problem solving. Some of this occurs when children are trying to figure out a process. For young children, a significant amount of the problem solving in project work occurs when children paint, build, draw, and construct representations.
Instructional Guideline 9: Metacognition	Activities stimulate metacognition and provide time for students to reflect and to "think about thinking." Students are given time to reflect and "consider new information . . . to maximize memory consolidation." Teachers "allow time for metacognition during class and to assign homework that requires metacognitive skills." End-of-day or end-of-class reflections or questions about content develop "habits of mind that encourage reflection." (p. 122)	The project process requires children to think about what they know about a topic and what they want to learn. The webbing process done by children and teacher together at the beginning of the project records their initial knowledge about the topic. Revisiting the web throughout the process focuses children on what they have learned in their investigation and what more they might want to learn. Re-creating a web at the end of the project enables them to reflect on what and how much they have learned. Reviewing progress on the project in discussions in both large and small groups enables ongoing reflection.
Instructional Guideline 10: Learning Throughout the Life Span	Skills are taught "at an appropriate time based on the characteristics of the learner." "Developmentally appropriate age-related activities should be milestones and benchmarks, not roadblocks." Students who don't meet the standard developmental milestones are not labeled. "Be sure the student understands that he can improve, but only with effort; the student's willingness to do better is crucial to improvement. " (pp. 123–124)	In project work children can contribute at their current skill level but are continually challenged to reach beyond typical expectations by the open-ended nature of investigation and representation. A 3-year-old is often seen creating signs for constructions, a process that motivates them to write and learn about letters. Children role-play adult work in the project process (e.g., a waiter taking orders for pizza or a real estate agent interviewing a customer wanting to buy a house). Children learn to write large numbers because they want to record them. In project work, children often attempt difficult tasks, such as designing a play car that they can get in and pretend to drive. A common experience is for first attempts to fail, and another way to figure out what went wrong and another way to do a task.

Note: Content from *The New Science of Teaching and Learning: Using the Best of Mind, Brain, and Education Science in the Classroom*, by T. Tokuhama-Espinosa, 2010, pp. 114–124.

Changes in the Brain

It might be helpful here to focus on how the brain does change. One of the agreed-upon principles of MBE Science is that *"the brain is a complex, dynamic, and integrated system that is constantly changed by experience though most of this change is only evident at a microscopic level"* (Tokuhama-Espinosa, 2010, p. 101; emphasis added). Whenever children learn something new, the brain creates connections between neurons (cells) in the brain. When the cells connect, they create networks of neurons. These neuronal networks are built individually by each child through the experiences that the child has. Catherwood (2000), in a review of young children's growth and development and brain research, concluded that

> experiences that support the child in making connections amongst domains of knowledge (e.g. as in "event-based" programmes in which children develop activities around conceptual themes such as topics) are likely to impact on and enhance the richness of these neural networks in the child's brain. (p. 33)

Squire and Kandel (2009) describe these networks as *engrams*. It might be helpful to think about the creation of engrams as building roads, or more accurately building a network of roads such as the interstate highway system. As the roads are used, we improve them, making them bigger and stronger, adding to and extending into other new roads. Unlike the interstate highway system, these roads, however, are more like forest paths. When the path is not used for a long time or used infrequently, it begins to disappear and is no longer readily available for new experiences to connect to them.

This natural biological process of growing and pruning back enables the brain to adapt to its environment. The process is similar to how one would shape a bonsai tree, only instead of using scissors to prune and shape, the brain is shaped by use. What is used remains, and what is not used is pruned. The result is a change in density of the neuronal structure of the brain. Learning something creates physical change in the brain. Some of those changes can actually be seen by

examining the brain with new technologies. One study looked at changes caused by learning to juggle (Draganski et al., 2004). Learning to juggle changed the density (connections of neurons) of a specific section of the brain. Failing to continue to practice juggling, however, resulted in a decrease of density, confirming that use is important. This shaping process has been identified as a theoretical principle called *canalization*. Just as the flow of a river becomes shaped and restricted when levees are added to the banks of the river to create a canal, so too in brain development canalization refers to the idea that as development proceeds, the originally great range of behavioral potentials or plasticity narrows (Blair, 2002; Kuo, 1976). This enables the brain to become more efficient at doing what it most often needs to do and less efficient at what it no longer is called upon to do. Each individual has a brain development history, which in fact makes the brain more efficient in its environment but also narrows the range of possibilities as that individual develops.

In a way similar to the jugglers, when a child learns something or masters a new skill, the actual physical structure of the brain has changed. According to Hardiman (2012) and Blair (2002), the building of these neuron pathways is affected by emotions, attention, prior knowledge, and the degree of rehearsal or repeated learning. The more a pathway is used, the stronger and more efficient it becomes, but it is almost as important for teachers to remember that the building of these efficient strong pathways develops a readiness for new skills and new knowledge, just as building a new highway is often followed by new communities along that highway. We also see this idea of brain shaping in the following MBE Science principle: *"All brains are not equal in their ability to solve all problems. Both context and ability influence learning. Context includes the learning environment, motivation for the topic of new learning, and prior knowledge"* (Tokuhama-Espinosa, 2010, p. 100; emphasis added). The importance of environment, engaging topics, and beginning with prior knowledge are ways that teachers shape children's intellect. If experience shapes the brain, it is worth asking, what are the brains of children in classrooms being shaped to do? What kind of experiences should children have in early schooling?

Each Brain—Unique

The uniqueness of a child's brain is an important understanding for teachers. According to the first MBE Science principle, "*Human brains are as unique as faces; while the basic structure is the same, no two brains are identical. Despite general patterns of organization in how different people learn and which brain areas are involved, each brain is unique and uniquely organized*"(Tokuhama-Espinosa, 2010, p. 99; emphasis added). Instructional methods that do not provide alternative ways for children to learn and do not take into consideration the prior experiences of children are less likely to be effective.

Although each brain is unique, there are similarities in how the brain processes information that can be helpful for teachers, especially those learning to guide project work (Sousa, 2010). Four areas of the brain function in the processing of information (Zull, 2002):

- The sensory and postsensory cortex gets information.
- The temporal integrative cortex near the sensory cortex makes meaning of information.
- The frontal integrative cortex creates new ideas from these meanings.
- The motor cortex acts on those ideas.

The parts of the brain that are used become more efficient and better able to function. According to Zull (2002), "If teachers provide experiences and assignments that engage all four areas of the cortex, they can expect deeper learning than if they engage fewer regions. The more brain areas we use, the more neurons fire and the more neural networks change—and thus the more learning occurs" (p. 5). In other words, if teachers provide children with rich sensory experiences and opportunities to make sense of information for themselves, create new ideas, and then act on those ideas, teachers will be enabling children to use those areas of the cortex and empowering them with a better-functioning brain.

It would be a mistake, however, to focus too much on separate areas of the brain and their functions as happened in the development of neuromyths such as right-brain versus left-brain thinking. Sylwester (2005) provides a helpful kitchen metaphor for how the brain works. The brain functions similarly to the way a kitchen functions. In a kitchen food is received, stored, and processed. Kitchen utensils enable a variety of menus, but all utensils are not used all the time. A recipe is a record of what provisions and tools have been used to prepare the food and what will be needed to prepare it again. Similarly, the brain receives, integrates, and stores information from inside and outside the body. It is processed in a variety of ways. A brain scan records which brain areas are involved in the activity and what occurred. As in a kitchen where combinations of food, seasonings, and utensils are endless, so can the brain organize and process in a multitude of ways. The brain is a master at integration and that integration is focused on making meaning of experiences. Zull (2011) summarizes it in this way: "We gather new information, think about it; identify categories and relationships, engage with it in creative ways and eventually we understand" (pp. 88–89).

An important implication from this description of how the brain functions is that integration takes time. There has to be time to connect new information with previous experiences, to reflect on it, to sort it out, and to apply it in a variety of ways. Through this process, true understanding of concepts and processes develops. Sometimes this understanding occurs instantly but more often over a longer period of time. Connections gradually occur with a multitude of other experiences resulting in deep learning, which is more likely to persist and more likely to become a foundation for later learning. We will revisit this concept of shaping and brain areas in later chapters when we discuss different aspects of project work.

Young Children's Brains

In addition to our general understanding of how the brain develops and functions, research specifically on the brains of young preschool children is also helpful for teachers to know about. When children enter into the preschool years, the cerebral cortex is not fully developed (Copple, 2012). Some of the challenges in thinking for very young preschoolers include solving problems, focusing attention and concentrating (especially for long periods of time), and learning and applying strategies for remembering. These thinking abilities can develop during the preschool years when there are experiences that children find significant and meaningful, especially if these can be revisited through play (Berk, Mann, & Ogan, 2006).

Children of this age are more likely to remember "scripts" than lists. This is one reason that play is so helpful for cognitive development for preschool children. When planning and participating in their own play scripts based on their own experiences, such as the trip to the seed store, they are able to remember, problem-solve, and create new meanings.

The preschool years are also when significant gains occur in the child's ability to use symbolic thinking, to choose something to represent something else. During this period of time there is "an extraordinary increase in children's ability to mentally or symbolically represent concrete objects, action and events" (Copple, 2012, p. 17).

During the preschool years children are more able to reason and solve problems when they understand why things are the way they are. For example, they can understand why different seeds are necessary to attract a variety of birds and how the bird's beak determines what seeds it can process. Of significant use to the cognitive development of young children is the opportunity to ask questions and find answers by connecting with adults and others who can assist them (Chouinard, 2007).

If the brain is shaped by experiences and if young children can have experiences that enable them to think deeply, ask questions, encounter and solve problems, and learn how to represent what they are learning symbolically, they will develop a brain ready for more complex learning and be more successful in later schooling. These mind- and brain-building experiences are unlikely to happen when children's learning experiences are passive and consist mainly of adults transmitting facts using predetermined scripts. Although young children can be taught to recognize letter shapes and sounds through drill and practice and to repeat facts, these are small accomplishments compared with the ability of their brains to create individual scripts, to come up with their own solutions to problems, and to create complex representations that emerge from their own understanding of how things work. There is danger in focusing on small, discrete, and testable skills at the expense of developing the underlying ability of the brain to seek meaning and to integrate experiences into complex understandings.

My favorite analogy to explain the importance of developing mind and brain capacity in the early years is a comparison of my husband's restored antique sports car and a new car designed for today's highways. This is the difference between *tinkering* and *automotive engineering*. My husband has spent hours restoring a 1949 Crosley Hotshot convertible. It took an enormous amount of tinkering—working on this part, then that part, adjusting a little here and a little there—to get the original motor to peak functioning. He has brought the car from not being able to start at all to being able to go about 45 miles an hour. We love to drive it on the lanes and small highway near our home; however, we will never drive it on the interstate highway. It is too slow and lacks the power to compete with the bigger cars and trucks that roar down the four lanes of the interstate. To get that car ready for the superhighway, to be powerful and fast enough for those speeds, would require an automotive engineer to design a new engine; it is unlikely that tinkering would ever do it. I believe that for the last decade in public education, we have focused on *tinkering*, on subskills and testable concepts.

What we educators should be doing is thinking like automotive engineers and planning learning experiences for children, especially those who face challenges, that will enable them to develop the mind and brain capacity to run on the superhighways of the 21st century, not limiting them to the byroads of the future The more children think, the more they are capable of thinking. The more deeply children think, the greater the probability that they will be able to do deep thinking in the future. Educators should be building a better motor rather than tinkering. They should be building a physiological foundation for lifetime learning and higher-order thinking.

FOUNDATIONS OF PROJECT WORK

In this chapter we looked at the new field of Mind, Brain and Education Science and how project work, such as Michelle's Seed Store Project, is consistent with the instructional guidelines coming from this new field. Much of the explanations in this chapter have focused on the "B" (Brain) of MBE, or the neuroscience perspective. However, as we have learned from MBE Science, effective education for the 21st century cannot be based on neuroscience alone. That mistake was made in the 1990s with specific "brain-based" strategies, some of which have now been identified as neuromyths.

The fields of psychology (mind and behavior, the "M" in MBE) and pedagogy (individual education and learning, or the "E" in MBE) have a rich history of studying learning through observations, hypothesizing and testing hypotheses, and experimenting.

Figure 1.9. How Mind, Brain, and Education Science Influences Experiences for Young Children

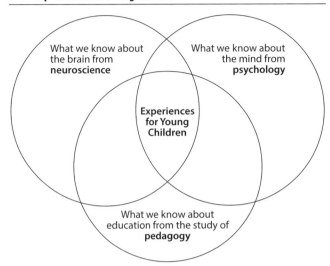

When combined with the insights from neuroscience, these can provide a context and methodology for effective teaching and learning (see Figure 1.9). The project approach to curriculum comes from these fields. Chapter 2 focuses on the psychological and pedagogical foundations of project work. Reviewing the rich tradition of these fields provides a foundation for specific strategies teachers can use to deepen project work and thereby help children develop their mind and brain capacity.

Supporting the Development of the Mind Through Deep Project Work

I began Chapter 1 with a description of Michelle Fernandes's classroom. When Michelle and her students learned about seeds and created their play seed store, they were involved in an investigation called a *project*. In guiding this investigation, Michelle used strategies and methods of the *project approach*. These strategies and methods are consistent with the instructional guidelines from MBE Science provided in Chapter 1. Incorporating findings from the fields of psychology and education, these guidelines can also assist teachers in making project work more productive. In this chapter, I draw insights from these fields to understand the foundations of the project approach and deepen children's learning.

INSIGHTS FROM PSYCHOLOGY

The Concept of Intelligence

In education, we are in the business of developing children's intellect. This includes the capacity for rational and intelligent thought and the power to understand and deliberately acquire knowledge, especially higher, more complex knowledge. We want children to fulfill their potential and be able to attain their life goals. In the past when teachers talked about intelligence, it was usually defined by performance on an intelligence test or an IQ score. Gardner (2006) discusses at length our changing view of intelligence, rejecting the single IQ score and advocating for a broader, less restricting concept based on a person's ability not just to acquire but to understand and use what he has learned in new contexts. Gardner focuses on an individual's ability to function in his society rather than on what he knows: "I define intelligence as the ability to solve a problem, or to fashion a product which is valued in at least one culture" (p. 133).

Throughout the principles and instructional guidelines of MBE there is an emphasis on "doing," on active learning. We want children to be able to think and experience accomplishments. This requires opportunities and practice, both of which can occur in project work.

Executive Function

In addition to recognizing changing views of intelligence, researchers are focusing on the construct of the brain's *executive function* (EF). Executive function is not just a single activity of the brain or a single way of thinking. Instead, it is an interconnection of processes. Executive function includes problem solving, reasoning, and planning. This processing occurs largely in the prefrontal cortex (Blair, 2008). According to Blair and Razza (2007), executive function is more important for school readiness than is intelligence quotient. Executive functioning predicts math and reading competence throughout all school years (Gathercole, Pickering, & Stegmann, 2004). EF also includes the processes of maintaining information in working memory, inhibition, shifting and sustaining attention, and goal-directed action (Blair, 2008). It develops rapidly in early childhood.

Especially important is the development of self-regulation, or the ability to manage oneself. Self-regulation skills include the ability to manage emotions, to control bodily functions, and to maintain focus and attention (Gillespie & Seibel, 2006). Children begin to develop self-regulation in infancy and continue to develop it as they learn to follow rules and to inhibit actions in social interactions (Blair, 2003). The most difficult kind of EF and the last to develop is cognitive self-regulation, or the regulation of one's own thinking processes. Cognitive self-regulation appears in 4-year-olds as they develop their ability to plan (e.g., what they are going to do in learning centers) and utilize proper responses (e.g., listening when a story is read) (Rice, 2012).

Teachers and others concerned about the education of children in the 21st century have become interested in the development of executive function. Many believe, as I do, that success in the future will require creativity, flexibility, self-control, and discipline.

> Children will need to think creatively to devise solutions never considered before. They will need working memory to mentally work with masses of data and see new connections among elements, flexibility to appreciate different perspectives and take advantage of serendipity, and self-control to resist temptations and avoid doing something they would regret. (Diamond & Lee, 2011, p. 959)

These processes of executive function determine how aware a child is of her emotions and the choices she makes regarding her behavior. Executive function is important for school and life success. Beginning early in life, a child's ability to attend and focus, to set goals, and to follow through establish a trajectory of development. Executive function enables the building of a foundation for cognitive skills and acquiring new meaningful knowledge. Classrooms that focus primarily on acquisition of knowledge facts and on drill and practice of letters and numbers, without providing opportunities for children to develop and practice the processes of executive function, may actually

negatively impact children's school success. According to Blair (2003),

> A premature focus on knowledge acquisition in preschool without attention to cognitive and social–emotional competencies through which knowledge is acquired could lead to learning problems and early school failure for some children. (p. 3)

As children leave preschool and enter kindergarten and the early primary grades, these cognitive and social–emotional competencies become even more important as children take on increasing responsibility for focusing, directing, and persisting in their learning process. Moran and Gardner (2010) coined the phrase "hill, skill, and will" in explaining the critical role of executive function. When children are able to integrate what they want to accomplish (the hill) with what they can do (skill), and direct their energy to accomplishing goals they set (the will), they are developing the processes of executive function. In other words, children must develop the ability to set their own goals and to learn and then use skills for achieving those goals, and have the commitment and persistence to work toward goals. EF develops over time beginning in early childhood and continuing into early adulthood. The good news is that executive function processes can be taught and practiced. Figures 2.1 and 2.2 show executive function skills in action in the Seed Store Project.

Child initiation and child direction, which is an integral part of project work, provide opportunities for children to practice hill, skill, and will. The social nature of project work requires children to collaborate and cooperate. Teachers who regularly include project work in their classroom often comment that they expend time and effort on projects because they see so much growth in children's ability to focus and persist.

The development of executive functioning in children requires practice, and project work is one way that opportunities for practice can be provided while still accomplishing curriculum goals. Understanding the importance of executive function and making sure that many opportunities exist in

Figure 2.1. Creating the plan for the classroom seed store as this child is doing requires goal setting, communication with others, and the use of symbolic tools.

Figure 2.2. When children decide to create a group structure such as the seed store, they are setting their own goals, practicing many skills, and experiencing the results of hard work and persistence—hill, skill, and will.

project work for children to exercise EF skills is a way that teachers can deepen project work. In the chapters in Part II, specific strategies for accomplishing this will be presented.

Learning as a Sociocultural Experience

Additional insight from the field of psychology comes from the work of Lev Vygotsky (1896–1934) and others who developed *sociocultural theory*. Instead of viewing education as acquisition of skills and knowledge for each individual subject, sociocultural theory focuses on the contributions of social and cultural experience to the development of the child. I have found three concepts from Vygotsky's sociocultural theory to be especially meaningful for teachers guiding project work:

- The concept of psychological tools
- The role of mediation or social interaction in learning
- The zone of proximal development

According to sociocultural theory, a high-quality learning experience is one that assists children in developing basic cognitive (thinking) skills and metacognitive skills (monitoring and thinking about your own thinking). These thinking skills apply to all areas of the curriculum, enabling children to do higher-level thinking across areas such as math, science, or literature (Kozulin, Gindes, Ageyev, & Miller, 2003).

Psychological Tools. In Vygotsky's sociocultural theory, "psychological tools are those symbolic systems specific for a given culture that when internalized by individual learners become their inner cognitive tools" (Kozulin et al., 2003, p. 3). Let us examine the components of this statement. A *tool* is something one uses to accomplish a task or perform a process. Think about a hammer or a washing machine. A hammer enables us to drive a nail into a wall. A washing machine enables us to accomplish the goal of washing our clothes. The difference between psychological tools and tools such as hammers and washing machines is that using a hammer or washing machine does not change the tool or its user; it simply enables the task to be accomplished. A hammer is still just a hammer whether it strikes a nail or not.

The tools Vygotsky refers to are *psychological tools* or *mind tools*. These tools include symbolic systems that have been created by others and passed on. Letters and numbers that enable one to read, write, and do calculations are examples of mind tools. According to Alex Kozulin (2003), "psychological tools are those symbolic artifacts—signs, symbols, texts, formulae, graphic organizers—that when internalized help individuals master their own natural psychological functions of perception, memory, attention, and so on" (pp. 15–16).

These tools help the mind accomplish meaningful tasks and perform certain processes, but while in use, they also shape the development of the mind, enhancing and expanding the possible ways of thinking that each mind can do. We know from neuroscience that this shaping creates physical changes in the brain. Internalizing psychological tools enables thinking to happen and builds capacity for future thinking. The use of the tool (such as reading and writing) becomes a vehicle for development.

There are two important implications from this concept of psychological tools that shape thinking capabilities:

1. Symbolic systems such as reading and writing should be viewed as tools that build children's mind and brain capacity for learning. Integration of these tools into project work will benefit children, especially when they are introduced as tools for accomplishing children's goals in their project work. In contrast, teaching these symbolic systems devoid of their use as tools is less likely to serve that role of driving development. For example, approaching literacy by having children memorize a letter a week is unlikely to be as effective as providing experiences where children are motivated to learn specific letters so they can do work that is important to them (i.e., to decipher words on seed packets, make labels for bins, and create signs for their store). Projects that are rich in opportunities for children to use tools (such as the ability to read words) within the context of the children's own goals will be more effective for cognitive growth.

2. Anticipating and planning what and where these psychological tools might be needed within a project will increase the ability of that project to develop mind and brain capacity of children. Project work should not be thought of as a separate curriculum experience that must be squeezed into a busy schedule, but as an alternative way to accomplish math, literacy, scientific thinking, and so on.

Play offers an opportunity for young children to use psychological tools. In play they use objects to represent other objects and the language of the reality they have observed. Project work provides children with the motivation for rich play experiences, including opportunities to use language and the relationship with objects. At Discovery Preschool, in Peoria, Illinois, the Fire Truck Project in Pam Scranton's preschool classroom resulted in a child-designed fire truck complete with a steering wheel, buttons, and fire hoses—and deep sustained play (see Figure 2.3)

Mediation and Social Interaction. During learning experiences, social interaction (both teacher–child and child–child) enables children to learn how to use psychological tools. According to sociocultural theory, an effective teacher will observe children's attempts to use psychological tools and assist the child in learning how to use and apply them. Specific strategies the teacher might use are modeling, demonstrating, questioning, asking for clarification of children's thoughts, and assisting children in developing and executing plans. A number of terms are used to describe this role of the teacher, such as *mediating, scaffolding,* and *apprenticing.* For example, children may observe that the shoes of children in their class have different kinds of fasteners. In response to that interest, the teacher can assist children by showing them how they might classify and record that observation by using a chart, and then modeling for the class how to analyze the chart and form conclusions. In this way the children are apprentices and are learning by observing how the teacher does it. Are there more shoes that fasten by tying or by Velcro? By observing and responding to the children's interest, and then modeling and guiding them through this data-gathering process, the

Figure 2.3. According to Vygotsky (1933/1966), the features of play that support development include imaginary situations, the roles children act out, and the rules children follow while acting out their pretend scenarios.

teacher has provided them with a number of new psychological tools they can use (e.g., gathering and charting data, classifying). The next time there is an opportunity to gather data the children will be able to use this tool, eventually becoming totally independent in the process. There are many opportunities for learning about and using psychological tools in project work when children are investigating topics of interest. These are less likely to occur when children primarily complete worksheets or follow prescribed learning activities.

Zone of proximal development. One of the most widely recognized and used sociocultural constructs is the *zone of proximal development* set forth by Lev Vygotsky. Although Vygotsky's writing on this concept is sparse, others have applied the concept extensively and expanded it. Vygotsky chose the word *zone* because he conceived of development not as a point on a scale, but as a continuum of behaviors or degrees of maturation. By describing the zone as *proximal* (next to, close to), he meant that the zone is limited to those behaviors that will develop in the *near future* (Bodrova & Leong, 1996). In this description the term *near future* is key. Children should not be using their learning time doing over and over again tasks that they already can do; nor should children be asked to do tasks that are way beyond their understanding. A major goal of education should be to keep the work that we encourage children to do in their zone of proximal development where they are always learning and doing something they could not do before and the teacher provides support for that growth. This, of course, requires that the teacher be able to observe children in tasks in which their level of performance can be observed. When all children are creating the same craft or doing the same writing exercise, it is difficult to see what each child can already do and is capable of doing, or what is challenging. When project work provides many opportunities for children to self-select the work they do and many opportunities for individuals and small groups to set their own goals, the teacher can more easily see where each child is regarding development of these psychological tools. The teacher can then

structure the task and the environment and adjust the amount of adult intervention based on each child's current level of development or the child's zone of proximal development. In the Seed Store Project, when labels for seed bins were needed, some children created a label by copying the word that Michelle wrote for them, some children wrote the word as Michelle dictated the letters, and some children were able to write the word independently by carefully making the letters they heard as they said the word to themselves. Some of the younger 3-year-olds had no interest in making signs. By identifying the zone of proximal development, Michelle was able to encourage each child to approach the task in a way that was neither too easy nor too difficult. In the project, individual children were able to approach the task within their zone of proximal development.

Play

Vygotsky (1933/1966) valued play, calling it the leading-edge activity for development in the early years:

A child's greatest achievements are possible in play, achievements that tomorrow will become his average level of real action. . . . (p. 21)

In play a child is always above his average age, above his daily behavior; in play it is as though he were a head taller than himself. As in the focus of a magnifying glass, play contains all developmental tendencies in a condensed form; in play it is as though the child were trying to jump above the level of his normal behavior (pp. 25–26).

Dramatic or make-believe play where children manipulate objects, plan sequences, and act out real situations or events is typical of children in preschool and early primary school. This play enables children to use symbolic tools in meaningful ways. Vygotsky (1933/1966) emphasizes the importance of dramatic play as opposed to other kinds of play. Bodrova (2008) describes Vygotksy's differentiation as "real" play, or play that shapes development. This play has three major features:

children create an imaginary situation, they take on and act out roles, and they make and follow a set of rules determined by specific roles.

"Real" play, as Vygotsky describes it, is a common component of project work at this age level. In observing project work in classrooms across the country, I have seen how children use what they have learned in their investigations to create play environments such as stores, garages, farms, hospitals, and so on. Children incorporate what they have learned about a topic in using symbolic tools and higher order mental functions. The Seed Store in Michelle's classroom is an example of one of those play experiences. The children created their own store and pretended to be customers, seed preparers, and clerks. They developed "rules" regarding how one approaches the store and asks for seed and who plays what roles in the process of selling the seed. As they acted out the roles they had observed during their investigation, they performed tasks (such as finding the requested kind of seed) they had observed adults do and used the same vocabulary. All through this process they were able to practice and use psychological tools in gratifying ways (see Figure 2.4).

Levels of Thinking

In addition to a concept of intelligence, executive function, and the sociocultural nature of learning, the science of psychology has also provided us with a way to think about different forms of thinking. Educational psychologist Benjamin Bloom worked with a group of colleagues to develop a "taxonomy" or classification system of thinking that could be used in writing goals and objectives (Bloom & Krathwohl, 1956). The result was a six-tiered model for classifying thinking arranged in order of complexity. On the bottom three levels were *knowledge, comprehension*, and *application*. The upper three levels were *analysis, synthesis*, and *evaluation*. About 50 years later, a new group of psychologists revised the taxonomy based on education needs for the 21st century to make it more usable for a wider audience (Anderson & Krathwohl, 2001). The new terminology uses action verbs and places *creating* at the highest level of

Figure 2.4. When playing in their seed store, children use academic tools, practice new vocabulary, and experience the rewards of their persistence and hard work.

thinking. As a hierarchy, the levels of thinking are arranged in order from lowest to highest with each level including and building on those below:

- *Remembering:* Retrieving, recognizing, and recalling relevant knowledge from long-term memory
- *Understanding:* Constructing meaning from oral, written, and graphic messages through interpreting, exemplifying, classifying, summarizing, inferring, comparing, and explaining
- *Applying:* Carrying out or using a procedure through executing, or implementing
- *Analyzing:* Breaking material into constituent parts, determining how the parts relate to one another and to an overall structure or purpose through differentiating, organizing, and attributing
- *Evaluating:* Making judgments based on criteria and standards through checking and critiquing
- *Creating:* Putting elements together to form a coherent or functional whole; reorganizing elements into a new pattern or structure through generating, planning, or producing (pp. 67–68)

Infants and toddlers primarily use the first two levels (remembering and understanding), but by age 6 most children are able to think using all six levels. Bloom's taxonomy is most helpful for teachers doing project work as an aide to planning, providing, and evaluating project work so they can be sure that children are experiencing different kinds of thinking. Considering what we know from other fields, it is probably less helpful to focus on the sequence of the levels of thinking. There are some that come in a logical order. *Remembering* something is a prerequisite of *understanding* something, and understanding is a prerequisite for *applying* what one remembers and understands. For example, a child must be able to remember and understand the purpose of the seed mixing machine before he can apply that knowledge to using one in play. However, the higher-order thinking skills of *analyzing, evaluating,* and *creating* at this age level are more likely to happen simultaneously or in varying order. A new taxonomy developed by Marzano and Kendall (2006) also emphasizes doing or action, and they maintain that their taxonomy is not hierarchical, which is more consistent with what we now understand of brain processing. This newer taxonomy also calls attention to metacognition.

Considering what we know from other fields such as neuroscience, learning is much more complex than both of these taxonomies imply. Complex learning experiences require many types of thinking, and these are integrated and connected in many different ways. However, the revised Bloom taxonomy by Anderson and Krathwohl (2001) is familiar to most educators, and it provides a structure for thinking and communicating about the provision of opportunities for thinking in their classrooms. But it must be recognized that there is a difference in quality of thinking. Lower-level thinking and higher-level thinking, even though not in a lockstep hierarchy, are distinguishable. One of the most important implications for project work is that the higher levels of thinking must rest upon and build on the lower levels. As I discussed in Chapter 1, the development of memory in young children—that is, the ability to recall and revisit what they have learned—is very important. It would be a mistake to think that project work is only about higher-level thinking. Children must have something to think about! Remembering, recognizing, and recalling knowledge; summarizing, classifying, and comparing; and repeating simple procedures and processes they observed are important aspects of deep project work. The children in Michelle's classroom developed a strong knowledge base about seeds and the seed store before they were able to analyze what they needed to create their classroom seed store, make plans, evaluate their plans, and then create the seed store.

Another important implication from both taxonomies is that learning experiences should not be limited to memorizing, explaining, and carrying out procedures. There must be opportunities for higher-level thinking to occur. As the children explored and investigated seeds and the seed store, Michelle observed what aspect of the world of seeds the children were most interested in. This project could have gone in any number of directions: a bird feeder project, a seed project, or even a plant-growing project. In empowering the children to follow their interest, she enabled the children to experience the higher levels of thinking. If Michelle had decided in advance that this project would result in a seed store or if she had planned the seed store for them and created it in the dramatic play area, the thinking experiences of the children would have remained at lower levels. Project work has the potential to provide opportunities for children to do thinking at all levels.

In addition to revising the hierarchy of levels of thinking, Marzano and Kendall (2006) call attention to different types of knowledge or knowing. They identify four categories of knowledge:

- Factual Knowledge—terminology, specific details, and elements
- Conceptual Knowledge—classifications and categories, principles and generalizations, theories, models, and structures
- Procedural Knowledge—subject-specific skills and algorithms, subject-specific techniques and methods, criteria for determining when to use appropriate procedures
- Metacognitive Knowledge—strategies for thinking, cognitive tasks, self-knowledge

In their Seed Store Project, the children learned a great number of facts about seeds. They learned how to classify seeds and feeders. They learned all about how seed mixtures are made and how they could create their own seed mixture based on the preferences of different birds. They also developed self-knowledge regarding their own ability to investigate a problem and work out a solution with others, and as we can see from Nolan's comment in Chapter 1, they also learned about how they felt when they worked hard. In the chapters in Part II, Bloom's revised taxonomy and these four categories of knowledge from Marzano and Kendall will be helpful as we look at strategies for developing projects into learning experiences that include opportunities for higher-level thinking.

INSIGHTS FROM PEDAGOGY

The field of psychology has provided some key understandings from the study of the mind and behavior to establish a foundation for deep project work. In this section, the focus is the project approach itself. My experiences in training teachers in project work have led me to believe that deep project work is more likely to happen in classrooms when teachers have a clear vision of the origin and purposes of the project approach.

Development of the Project Approach

The project approach is derived from a tradition of hands-on, child-directed, investigative learning. Most scholars who write about project work and its many forms (Edutopia, 2014; Glassman & Whayley, 2000; Helm & Katz, 2011; Katz & Chard, 2000; Markham, Larmer, & Ravitz, 2003) credit John Dewey's work at his experimental laboratory school at the University of Chicago, 1896–1904, for articulating the basic concept now known as a project. (Dewey's contributions are discussed in more detail later in this chapter.) Projects were a major component of the Progressive Education Movement that grew out of Dewey's work. Although interest in project work waned in the 1950s, it surfaced again in the 1960s and 1970s, when early childhood teachers and administrators traveled from the United States to observe British Infant Schools

in England, where project work was an important part of the curriculum (L. Smith, 1997). It was there that Lilian Katz observed project work and began to think and write about projects. It was there also that I, at the beginning of my career, observed project work in a delightful infant school in London. In 1989, interest in the potential of project work was renewed in the United States with the publication of the first edition of *Engaging Children's Minds: The Project Approach* (Katz & Chard, 1989).

There are many variations of project work. Variations usually come from differences in the developmental ages of students and age-level variations in their skills. Project work in a preschool classroom like Michelle's with children who are beginning to learn about the world of literacy looks significantly different from project work in a 5th-grade classroom where students use literacy as a research tool. The ability to proficiently read and write enables older children to use the Internet for research, read and analyze original written materials, and create written reports (Boss & Krauss, 2007). These differences affect how children investigate, research, and represent their learning. Even though there are variations, there are consistent characteristics that differentiate projects from other approaches to curriculum. Thomas (2000) summarizes criteria that distinguish all project-based learning:

- Projects are central, not peripheral to the curriculum.
- Projects are not enrichment or add-on but a major component of the experience.
- Projects are focused on questions that drive students to explore and learn knowledge of a discipline (or content area).
- Projects involve students in a constructive investigation; that is, the project must involve the transformation and construction of new knowledge and new understandings.
- Projects are student-driven. They are not "teacher-led, scripted or packaged." Projects are authentic; they feel like explorations of real-life experiences. (Adapted from pp. 3–5)

Some variations of project work include *project-based learning* (Polman, 2000); *problem-based learning,* often called PBL (Barell, 2007); and *place-based education,* which centers investigations on the neighborhood and community near the school (G. A. Smith & Sobel, 2010). In all of these approaches to project work, learners are autonomous as they construct personally meaningful artifacts that are representations of their learning (Grant, 2002). Projects are described as *integrated* curriculum approaches because the investigative process integrates knowledge and skills across content areas. The project provides motivation for learning academic skills such as reading, writing, and scientific thinking, at the same time as it provides real-life opportunity to practice those academic skills. Another term used to describe project work is *constructivist learning* because children construct their own knowledge based on their investigation.

Project Work in Early Childhood

Project work is an especially good match to the developmental characteristics and skills of children during the early years of schooling (preschool, kindergarten, and primary grades). Interest in project work in early childhood was stimulated by impressive reports and displays of group projects conducted by children in the preprimary schools of Reggio Emilia, Italy (Edwards, Gandini, & Forman, 1993, 1998; Gandini, 1997; New, 1990; Rankin, 1992). According to Gandini (1997),

> Projects provide the backbone of the children's and teachers' learning experiences. They are based on the strong conviction that learning by doing is of great importance and that to discuss in group and to revisit ideas and experiences is the premier way of gaining better understanding and learning. (p. 22)

Besides project work in the schools of Reggio Emilia, there are many variations of project work in early childhood education. The word *project* is used in a variety of ways by early childhood educators. Constructions by children of a model (such as a school bus) or a play environment (such as a shoe store) are sometimes called projects. Some teachers also use the term *project* to describe any learning experience that extends over several weeks even

though the learning experience may be completely teacher initiated and teacher directed. These learning experiences would not meet Thomas's criteria (2000) for project work described above. One way to distinguish project work from other learning experiences in preschool through primary grades is to ask these questions:

- Is this an investigation by children based on their own questions?
- Do the questions of the children determine the focus of the project (i.e., is it possible for an investigation of trees to change into a project on a lumber yard)?
- Do the children's questions during the project determine what happens next in the project?
- Are children using higher-level thinking skills such as hypothesizing, analyzing, and creating?
- Are children developing their own ideas, theories, and concepts?
- Are representations (such as play environments, models, artwork) planned and executed by the children?

The Seed Store Project in Michelle's classroom provides the experiences that are referred to in these questions. To guide the project, Michelle followed a specific process for using project work as an approach to curriculum called the *project approach* (see Helm & Katz, 2011). Other forms of project work for older-age students, such as problem-based learning and place-based learning, focus on content questions that are teacher or curriculum determined. In project work in the early years (pre-K through primary grades), I feel the project approach works well for guiding projects because the emphasis is on children's questions, which enables teachers to more easily match the developmental tasks and academic skill levels of young children.

Projects Versus Themes

In explaining the project approach to teachers, I find it helpful to compare and contrast project work with other curriculum approaches with which teachers may already be familiar. The project approach can be contrasted with units, themes, and learning centers, which are also ways to organize early learning experiences. A *theme* is an integrated learning experience focused on a broad concept or topic. Examples might include "winter" or "animals" or "the zoo." When using a theme, a teacher assembles books, photographs, and materials related to the theme. The teacher then plans activities related or connected to the theme in most content areas (such as language, math, or science). For example, in a thematic unit on the zoo, the teacher might read books about different animals in a zoo, and the children might watch a video about zoo animals. Children might make pictures of a zoo and even visit a zoo. *Units*, which have a narrower focus, usually consist of preplanned lessons and activities on a specific topic that teachers or a required curriculum consider important for the children to know about, such as magnets (Harlan, 1984). When using units, teachers or the curriculum decide the concepts and knowledge the children should learn. Many teachers also use *learning centers* to organize learning experiences in early childhood classrooms. Areas of the room are designated for the development of certain knowledge and skills, such as a "block area" or a "music and movement area" (Dodge, Colker, & Heroman, 2002). Materials and equipment for each area are selected to teach concepts and provide practice in skills that the teacher wants the children to develop.

Themes, *units*, and *centers* are usually teacher selected and teacher organized. These approaches to curriculum can be placed along a continuum as they vary in the degree of child initiation of the topic and the amount of involvement of the children in decision making (see Figure 2.5). Good teaching can occur all along the continuum. In fact, these approaches to curriculum often exist side by side in the same classroom with project work.

To further clarify the difference between project work and teacher-planned experiences, it might be helpful to think through an example. With a renewed interest in connecting children with nature, there are many early childhood programs and schools adding butterfly gardens to their outdoor areas. The planning and planting of such a garden has potential as a topic for either a *thematic unit* or *project work*. In a Butterfly Garden thematic unit, the teacher would introduce the topic; the children can plan the layout of the garden and then plant the garden and observe the results. They also may generate a list of questions about butterfly gardens. This learning experience, although valuable, is unlikely to meet the definition of a project.

Instead, a Butterfly Project might evolve in this way:

1. Children become interested in a butterfly in their play yard.
2. The teacher encourages the children to ask questions, which are recorded.

Figure 2.5. Degree of Child Initiation and Decision Making in Different Approaches to Teaching

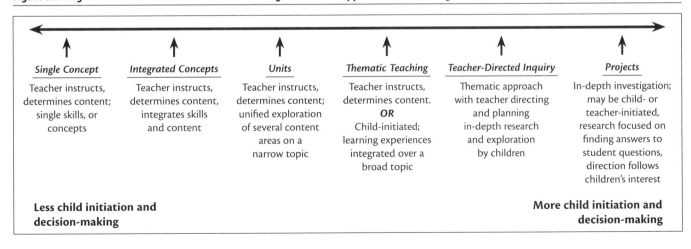

Single Concept	Integrated Concepts	Units	Thematic Teaching	Teacher-Directed Inquiry	Projects
Teacher instructs, determines content; single skills, or concepts	Teacher instructs, determines content, integrates skills and content	Teacher instructs, determines content; unified exploration of several content areas on a narrow topic	Teacher instructs, determines content. **OR** Child-initiated; learning experiences integrated over a broad topic	Thematic approach with teacher directing and planning in-depth research and exploration by children	In-depth investigation; may be child- or teacher-initiated, research focused on finding answers to student questions, direction follows children's interest

Less child initiation and decision-making   **More child initiation and decision-making**

3. Children engage in observations, which create more questions.
4. More butterflies are observed, and more questions are asked.
5. The teacher finds experts, who are interviewed by the children.

If a question is asked such as, "How can we get more butterflies?" this might result in more research, then the design and the planting of a butterfly garden. A Butterfly Project could then result in a new butterfly garden just as the thematic unit did; however, it could just as easily have become an investigation of caterpillars and how they turn into butterflies. It also could have resulted in a child-planned play about the life cycle of a butterfly, or a mural of butterflies, or a child-written encyclopedia of butterflies, or the creation of a giant butterfly model, or any number of representations. In the *project approach*, the direction of the project would be determined by child interest and engagement. It is the children's questions and what they found out that determine the direction and outcome of the project. Representations grow from the focus of the children's work. The simplest way for a teacher to check and see if a true project occurred in his classroom is to look at the role the children's questions played in the investigation:

- Were there meaningful questions?
- What happened as the result of those questions?
- How did children's learning shape their actions and representations?

If the role of questions was minimal in guiding the project work, then the experience would likely be more accurately described as a theme or a unit, rather than a project.

As interest in project work has increased, some publishers of curriculum materials have put together packages of materials for "project-like" experiences, sometimes referred to as *studies* or *investigations*. Although these are structured similarly to the project approach with webbing and questioning, they are more similar to themes and units than they are to project work. In these studies, topics are preselected, materials are preselected and often provided in a kit, and goals and activities are specified for the teacher. Although I once saw a teacher use a prepared study to explore a topic and then have a deep project develop based on children's interest, my experience is that this does not happen very often. The studies that I have observed were not what I would call deep investigations either for the teacher or the children.

I find that teachers are more likely to have rich project work in their classroom when they base the project on observations of children's deep interests as seen through their play, stories, and questions, which reveal their knowledge or their culturally based neural network. These teachers are still able to integrate and "cover" curriculum goals and concepts but do so in response to children's interests. The project is more likely to match the needs and culture of the children when the teacher chooses materials and plans experiences based on reflections about the children, as opposed to using preplanned kits. The purchase of kits can limit the direction of investigations that occur in a program and discourage teachers who are trying to connect to the intellectual life of their children. Since kits cost money, they are often used year after year regardless of the children's interest. Because teachers are not doing their own research, preparation, and planning, they are not as likely to become intellectually involved in the topic and develop their own rich background understandings of the topic. The result is that children don't have the opportunity to see their own teacher become an excited, committed colearner as he encounters new concepts and ideas right along with the children.

Although project work can provide a wealth of beneficial experiences for children, most teachers use project work along with themes and units. There are some topics that are important to discuss and share but that do not make good topics for deep investigation. Young children need to learn a lot of things, and many of these can be most efficiently and effectively taught through units or themes. These can build that necessary background knowledge and understanding on a broad number of topics. There are also skills such as literacy and numeracy that benefit from systematic instruction and teacher-determined activities.

There can be good and appropriate teaching all along the continuum in Figure 2.5; however, an early childhood classroom where all the learning experiences, day after day, are teacher directed and preplanned would more than likely not be considered scientifically substantiated teaching.

Project work, especially the project approach, can provide a structure, methods, and strategies that teachers can use to incorporate the instructional guidelines from MBE Science into their teaching. If you are not familiar with the project approach as used in prekindergarten and early primary grades, I urge you to consult *Young Investigators: The Project Approach in the Early Years* (Helm & Katz, 2011), which provides guidance for teachers using the project approach with children who are not yet proficient readers and writers. This can answer your basic questions about how to facilitate project work in classrooms with young children.

GUIDANCE FROM JOHN DEWEY ON PROJECT WORK

The project approach has evolved with practice and has been influenced by a variety of theorists and researchers from the fields of psychology and education. Although it is not possible in this book to document all the influences or to discuss all the contributions to project work, revisiting the work of John Dewey with what we now know from neuroscience may be especially useful for teacher reflection. Any teacher on a journey to deep project work would be wise to start with John Dewey, since, as pointed out earlier, the project approach as practiced in schools in the United States today is most commonly linked to his writings. He states his beliefs in *The School and Society* (1915), *Democracy and Education* (1916), *The Child and the Curriculum* (1928), and *My Pedagogic Creed* (1929), in addition to his many lectures and other writings. Although his earlier writings do not discuss projects, they provide insight into the theoretical foundation behind the structure, strategies, and methods of the project approach. Later writings,

specifically *How We Think* (1933), provide details of project work. Let us examine his key points related to projects.

The Primary Aim of Education

When teachers and parents describe project work, they often say that doing projects enables children to "learn how to learn." What they usually mean is that the experience of doing projects empowers students to develop skills that will enable them to become self-sufficient and manage their own learning needs in the future, to be efficient at the process of learning, and to be successful students in the future. Dewey describes this emphasis on development of a capacity for learning as the primary aim of education. Enabling children to build capacity to educate themselves is perhaps the main difference in outcomes between child-directed investigations, such as the Seed Store Project, and teacher-directed units, themes, and didactic instruction. According to Dewey (1916), "The aim of education is to enable individuals to continue their education— or . . . the object and reward of learning is continued capacity for growth" (p. 105).

Dewey contrasted his aim of education with the direct teaching of segregated content knowledge, which he believed led to a static education process with an unnatural separation between the activity the student engages in to reach the goal and the goal itself. Education, according to Dewey, should be viewed as dynamic and ongoing with the enhancement of the capacity to learn as the primary force in a child's education.

Some teachers in the field mistakenly describe project work as the opposite of "academic" learning; however, one of the reasons cited for doing project work is to provide a reason to learn academic skills and an opportunity to practice those academic skills in a meaningful way (Dewey, 1933; Helm & Katz, 2011; Katz & Chard, 1989). An integral component of building a capacity to learn is the building of academic skills such as reading, writing, scientific investigation, and numeracy. Project work, rather than being an alternative to academic learning, can become the vehicle for integration of academics. When planning for project work, remembering John Dewey's aim of education as the development of a long-term capacity and appetite for learning keeps the focus of a project experience on the child's capacity for growth. In other words, Dewey would consider more important what the children learn about how to investigate, organize, and plan during the Butterfly Project than the finished butterfly garden.

Nature of the Young Child

Dewey's description (1915) of the nature of the young child also provides a foundational understanding for project work. Dewey describes what he calls the *impulses* (or *instincts*) that drive the learning of children: the social instinct (which includes language and communication), the instinct of making (also called the constructive impulse), the instinct to investigate, and the expressive instinct (also called the art instinct).

Social Instinct. The *social instinct* of children is shown in "conversation, personal intercourse, and communication" (Dewey, 1915, p. 29). Children want to communicate with other children and adults. Young children are driven to connect their experiences, which are totally self-centered, to the experiences of others. This instinct to communicate is, according to Dewey (1915), "perhaps the greatest of all educational resources" (p. 29), and we should use it wisely. Project work is best done not in isolation but within a community of learners who converse and communicate about what they are learning. Teachers listening to and talking with children during the project process is important. A good example of project work that came directly from observations of children is the Camera Project in Lora Taylor's preschool classroom. This project began when Lora noticed what children were doing with a camera in the housekeeping area. As she observed their interest in the camera, she asked them questions. The camera became the focus of conversations between children. Children's conversations reveal not only their interests but also the challenges they are facing. Recording their thoughts and ideas and revisiting them as a group encourages development of communication skills and clarifies group ownership of the topic and project. Writing by the teacher or the children is an extension of that communication. For example, in the Camera Project children dismantled cameras to see how they worked and then created a word wall with illustrations of the parts and their names so that others could also learn them. (For more details about the Camera Project, see Helm & Katz, 2011, Chapter 6.)

Instinct of Making. The second instinct is one of making—the *constructive impulse*. Dewey, along with Vygotsky, found play to be important. Dewey believed that the constructive impulse first finds expression in play, in movement, gesture, and make-believe. As children create play environments such as post offices or stores, develop plays about what they are studying, and build elaborate, often large-size models or constructions such as a combine harvester or furnace, they confront and overcome problems. What materials should be used to make a door that will open and close? How can we make a steering wheel that will actually turn? It is when young children are making and doing that we see true investigation occur.

Instinct to Investigate. The third instinct Dewey discusses is the *instinct to investigate*, to find things out. According to Dewey, the instinct to investigate grows out of the combination of the constructive impulse with the conversational. Dewey describes this type of concrete investigation as the way young children learn, as opposed to conducting experiments that lead to abstract learning, such as understanding chemical processes, which have no meaning for young children. "The young child has not much interest for abstract inquiry" (p. 30). For example, in the Camera Project, after a field site visit, the children wanted to make a darkroom within their dramatic play area so they could pretend to develop photos as they had seen in a visit to an art guild studio. This caused a great deal of discussion between children about what should go into their darkroom and the correct sequence of the chemical development process.

Through discussion with one another and using the teacher and their notes as resources, the children remembered the sequence they had observed, the information the expert had shared, why each step occurred when it did, and how they should arrange their pretend developing trays. The exploration of sequence and eventual understanding came from the children's desire to create an authentic replica of the photographic darkroom, not from abstract interest in chemical processes. In this same way, in the hypothetical Butterfly Project, the desire to find a way to get more butterflies into their play yard could bring about the investigation of plants for a butterfly garden.

Expressive Instinct. The fourth impulse Dewey describes is the *expressive impulse,* the art instinct. Regarding young children, Dewey says, "the art instinct is connected mainly with the social instinct—the desire to tell, to represent" (p. 30). In project work in classrooms with young children we see this in the way their paintings, drawings, and sculptures represent their relationship with what they are studying. These usually are specific representations and may involve storytelling about the process. A painting of a butterfly as part of the Butterfly Project is more likely to be given a personal label ("the black one we saw on the yellow flower") than a scientific label.

Role of the Teacher

Dewey clarifies the teacher's role as facilitating and guiding the project process. In many aspects the teacher becomes a colearner in the project, another member of the community of learners. According to Dewey (1897), "The teacher is not in the school to impose certain ideas or to form certain habits in the child, but is there as a member of the community to select the influences which shall affect the child and to assist him in properly responding to those influences" (p. 9).

Dewey's philosophy of the role of the teacher and school was sometimes mistakenly described as one in which the child's interest of the moment is humored and children pursue whatever strikes their fancy. However, John Dewey's view of the role of the teacher is much more directive. In response to this concern, Dewey (1915) described the dilemma of following child interest and providing direction in this way:

> A question often asked is: If you begin with the child's ideas, impulses, and interests, all so crude, so random and scattering, so little refined or spiritualized, how is he going to get the necessary discipline, culture, and information? If there were no way open to us except to excite and indulge these impulses of the child, the question might well be asked. We should either have to ignore and repress the activities or else to humor them. But if we have organization of equipment and of materials, there is another path open to us. We can direct the child's activities, giving them exercise along certain lines, and can thus lead up to the goal which logically stands at the end of the paths followed. (p. 25)

Although the teacher is part of the community of learners, Dewey makes it clear that the teacher has a significant role in guiding a project: The teacher provides guidance through the organization of equipment and materials, providing access to experts, and supporting parts of project work in which children need assistance. He also alludes to the use of goals for project work. Another insight from Dewey pertains to the teacher's use of knowledge about child development and expectations for knowledge and skills of society to determine what aspects of the experience are most appropriate. Dewey (1933) provides specific advice for guiding projects: Activities should be adapted to the children's stage of development; they should have "the most ulterior promise as preparation for the social responsibilities of adult life"; and they should be maximally influential in "forming habits of acute observation and consecutive inference" (p. 44). Organization of the learning experience cannot occur in isolation of connection with the child. The role of the teacher is to have meaningful and frequent conversations with children, to listen carefully to their thoughts, questions, and concerns. The teacher must be a keen observer.

I believe that only through the continual and sympathetic observation of childhood's interests can the adult enter into the child's life and see what it is ready for, and upon what material it could work most readily and fruitfully. (Dewey, 1897, p. 29)

Decision Making in Project Work

In later years Dewey, in his writing and lectures, specifically described activities known as projects where students are involved in activities that require thinking as well as doing (Tanner, 1997). This later work provides insight for teachers when they are making critical decisions such as when to pursue or not pursue a topic, which experts and resources would be most valuable, or what materials and equipment would be most helpful. Dewey's insight is incorporated throughout books on the project approach.

Selection of Topics. Regarding topics, Dewey emphasized authentic explorations related to the occupations of adults in a democratic society. Dewey makes it clear that what children should be learning about and learning to do is authentic meaningful work. Project topics must be meaningful. According to Dewey (1897), "The child's own instincts and powers furnish the material and give the starting point for all education" (p. 20). Specifically regarding the nature of very young children, Dewey (1915) says,

We all know how self-centered the little child is at the age of four or five. If any new subject is brought up, if he says anything at all, it is: "I have seen that," or "My papa or mamma told me about that." His horizon is not large; an experience must come immediately to him, if he is to be sufficiently interested enough to relate it to others and seek theirs in return. (p. 29)

The implication of Dewey's work is that appropriate topics for project work would be topics that originate with the children's experience but link children to the real work of society and what it is that people do. An investigation of the pizza parlor down the street where the children and their families eat would be an appropriate project topic. Learning how to make their own pizzas, inventing their own kind of pizza, and building a play pizza parlor in their classroom are all learning experiences that might evolve in this investigation. In contrast, a topic such as Extinct Animals or the Costa Rican Rain Forest, although worthwhile topics for exploration at some point in children's lives, do not connect with either the world of young children or the work they see adults do. To ignore children's interest in their own immediate world would be noneducative according to Dewey (1897):

Save as the efforts of the educator connect with some activity which the child is carrying on of his own initiative independent of the educator, education becomes reduced to a pressure from without. It may indeed give certain external results, but cannot truly be called educative. (p. 20)

Role of Experts and Field Site Visits. Rich project investigations, especially those of very young children, bring them into contact with adults who are doing adult work. The involvement of adults in the investigations of young children is important. According to Dewey (1915):

Little children have their own observations and thoughts mainly directed toward people—what they do, how they behave, what they are occupied with and what comes of it. . . . Their interest is a personal rather than of an objective or intellectual sort. Their minds seek wholes, varied through episode, enlivened with action and defined in salient features–there must be go, movement, the sense of use and operation. (p. 88)

In Michelle's Seed Store Project, adults responded to children's interests by sharing what they knew about seeds. An employee at the local Kelly's Seed and Hardware Company showed how he uses a machine to sort and package different mixtures of seeds. In Lora Taylor's Camera Project, a photographer explained the components of a photo studio and helped the children take formal portraits. These are ways in which adults authentically use and relate to their world and the things in it. In the process of interviewing and interacting with these adults, children become energized and focused. I have observed many projects, in which children were losing interest in the topic and lacked clear goals, take on new life and purpose when the teacher brought the children into contact with adults whose occupation or hobby related to the topic. One of the teacher's roles in project work is to determine what, where, and with whom these interactions will occur.

Use of Artifacts in Project Work. In the Camera Project in Lora Taylor's preschool classroom, the dismantling of cameras and investigation of the differences between film cameras and digital cameras became a consuming interest of the children. They were motivated by their curiosity not only to investigate but also to write, draw, and discuss what they learned. The use of real objects and the investigation of authentic processes was an important consideration for Dewey. Tanner (1997) concluded that the biggest difference between learning experiences prescribed by Dewey and those occurring in kindergartens of that day could be captured in the word "real" (p. 31). Dewey was concerned that the tendency in kindergartens of his time, in the interest of being child centered, used materials that were artificial, that real things and real acts were not part of the child's world. Dewey instead thought that real things should make up the classroom; that imagination and imaginative play come through suggestions, reminiscences, and anticipations about the things the child uses. The more natural and straightforward these connections are, the more imaginative the child might be. For example, in a Pizza Project, Dewey would think it important that real pizza pans, oven paddles, and rolling pins be used rather than plastic replicas of pizzas or pots and pans made of brightly colored plastic (which even young children determine are not ovenproof) or those with eyes and faces on them.

Dewey has provided a fairly clear vision of what project work can be. There is an exercise in Appendix B for reflecting on Dewey's vision and your own project work

DIRECTION FROM LILIAN KATZ ON STRENGTHENING DISPOSITIONS

A review of the theoretical foundations of project work would not be complete without including the work of Lilian Katz and Sylvia Chard (1989, 2000) and their tireless support of the project approach. We will revisit their work numerous times throughout this book. I have always found Lilian Katz's guidance on *dispositions* to be especially helpful for teachers who are trying to deepen their project work. Katz (1993) distinguishes between academic tasks and intellectual goals Academic tasks in the early childhood curriculum usually address facts and skills that the majority of children are unlikely to learn spontaneously or by discovery, such as what a numeral means or what a letter represents. Intellectual goals relate to addressing dispositions—that is, habits of mind that include a variety of tendencies to interpret experience. Some of Katz's habits of mind include the disposition to

- Make sense of experience
- Theorize, analyze, hypothesize, and synthesize
- Predict and check predictions
- Find things out
- Strive for accuracy
- Be empirical
- Grasp the consequences of actions
- Persist in seeking solutions to problems
- Speculate about cause–effect relationships
- Predict others' wishes and feelings

According to Katz, the child may or may not have the willingness and commitment to think and act in these ways, and it is the role of teacher to support the strengthening of these dispositions. In some ways, there is a kinship between Howard Gardner's executive function of goal direction, commitment, and persistence and Katz's dispositions. Both agree that teaching academic facts and skills in isolation is not enough, and we would be wise to provide learning experiences for children that enable them to develop habitual ways of thinking and acting that contribute to their own intellectual development—to become young thinkers.

APPLYING WHAT WE'VE LEARNED

Facilitating deep project work can be challenging. Teachers who feel that their projects are not as effective or satisfying as they could be often conclude that the experience was more of a thematic unit than a project. The challenge is figuring out how to cross the line from rich thematic work to deep project work. In Part I of this book, knowledge from experts in the fields of neuroscience, psychology, and education was presented to create a foundation for teachers making decisions about how to guide projects. We will be revisiting this knowledge base in Part II as we move on to specific strategies and methods for facilitating deep project work.

Part II

STRATEGIES AND METHODS FOR DEEP PROJECT WORK

CHAPTER 3

Choosing the Best Topics

There are many decisions that teachers make when they are facilitating project work, but none is probably more important than deciding on the topic. This occurs during Phase I of the project. Figure 3.1 shows a flowchart of how a project, which follows the three-phase process of the project approach, typically progresses with young children. Following the exact sequence and structure on the project flowchart is not essential for project work to be successful; however, the flowchart does encourage a teacher to be thoughtful and reflective about the project process. Most deep project work that I have observed flows in this way.

Phase I is the period of time in which the project topic is selected (see Helm & Katz, 2011, Chapter 2). The teacher identifies a possible topic, builds his own background knowledge, and gathers information and resources on the topic. Phase I begins when the topic is first considered, and ends when the teacher has evaluated the children's prior knowledge, considered the curriculum goals and standards and how they might be integrated into the project, assisted the children in generating a list of worthwhile questions, and the class has made a commitment to investigate the topic.

In response to the Deepening Project Work Survey (described in the Introduction), teachers indicated that in their classrooms Phase I can last from a few days to 2 or 3 weeks. Sometimes a project topic emerges as a full-blown topic from children's spontaneous interest or an experience. The topic is selected, and the children are ready to investigate. More often, the selection of a topic is a gradual process. In the first phase of project work, a teacher recognizes a topic as a possible focus of project work, then provides learning experiences that build common knowledge and background experience.

All of the children become knowledgeable about the topic, rather than just a few knowing a great deal while most know very little.

When a teacher first identifies a topic of interest, that topic is often fairly broad and generalized. The teacher observes children's response to different aspects of the topic and their questions about it. As further exploration and discussion occurs, the project becomes focused on one or more aspects of the topic that appear to be of the most interest to the children. The direction the topic takes and the subsequent questions begin to shape the project into an investigation that engages the children and deeply involves them in research.

For example, suppose children saw a snake on their playground and watched as adults caught the snake. This was an event that captured the children's attention and led to numerous questions. Their teacher saw that the children quickly became emotionally involved in the experience. According to MBE Science, one way to develop mind and brain capacity is to utilize emotional involvement as motivation for study and investigation. When children are excited and feel positive about being able to learn what they want to learn, endorphins are released in the brain, which are a stimulant to the frontal lobes and produce a feeling of euphoria (Sousa, 2011). These strengthen memory retrieval and movement of short-term experiences into long-term memory. Learning experiences that capitalize on what children find emotionally interesting enables them to link emotions to content. All children in this classroom had the same experience of seeing the snake in its natural habitat and then observing it when it was relocated to an empty aquarium in the classroom. There was little need to build background knowledge, to make sure that all

Figure 3.1. The Three Phases of the Project Approach

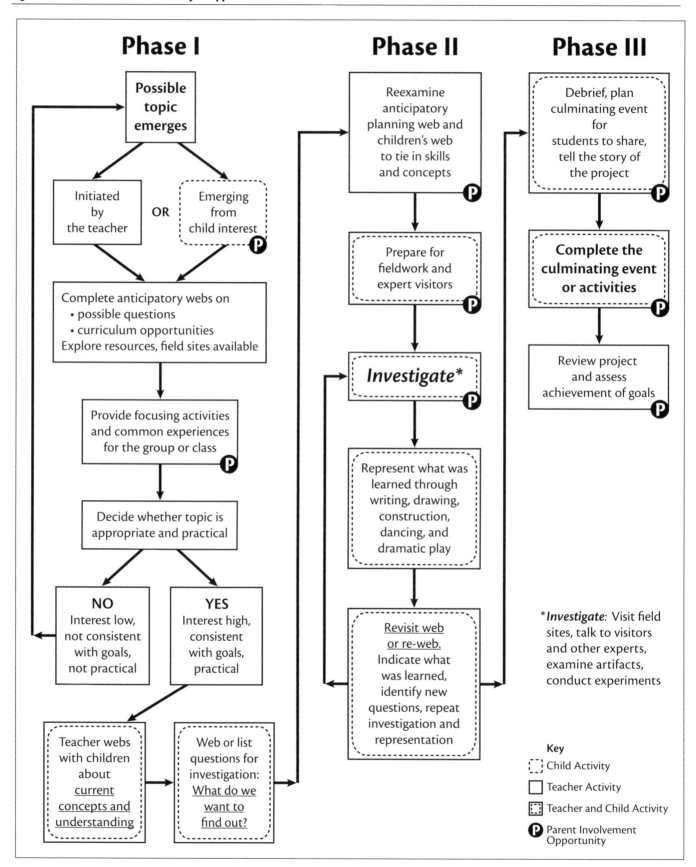

children in the classroom had experience with the topic before moving forward, or to create emotional involvement. Some topics, like the snake, emerge in this way, occurring spontaneously, falling into the lap of the teacher, or more precisely in this case, wriggling into the classroom, and creating intense interest. Phase I passes quickly with the recording of prior knowledge on a web and a list or web of children's questions.

THE IMPORTANCE OF THE TOPIC

Engagement is an essential component of project work. *Engagement* is defined as "holding the attention." Attention is important for building mind and brain capacity. It is one of those processes of executive function discussed in Chapter 2. If children do not pay attention during a learning experience, they are not thinking about that learning experience. (They could, of course, be thinking about many other things, such as Grandma coming to visit.) Attending enables children to develop memories and understand and apply what they are learning. These are the foundation for higher levels of thinking. Authentic engagement occurs when children have a genuine, not copied or pretend, interest in a topic. Authentic engagement can result in significant intellectual development in children. When the mind and brain are engaged, children exhibit a curiosity and enthusiasm for things related to the topic. The topic becomes a focus of their thinking as they read books, select artifacts, develop play themes, and create representations such as drawings, paintings, and constructions. Children engaged in a topic are also motivated to figure things out, to find solutions to problems, or to create something meaningful related to the topic. Thinking and using what they are learning to produce, create, and problem-solve enable them to develop intellectually.

Unfortunately, if a teacher chooses a topic that is not authentically engaging to the children, then subsequent project activities are also less likely to interest and engage them. This often results in the teacher having to "whip up" enthusiasm for the topic, to exaggerate her own interest, and

to create learning activities that she feels will be "fun" in order to keep the children's attention. For example, one teacher decided to do a project on shoes without genuine interest on the part of the children. Feeling the need to bring the children along, she had an idea of something to do that would be a great deal of fun, such as having children take off their shoes and socks and walk through paint onto a paper, resulting in a "mural" of children's footprints. This activity was an enjoyable sensory experience for children. Children noticed some things about their feet, primarily the different sizes of the footprints. The process, however, was tangentially related to the topic of shoes. It was the soles of children's feet that were captured in the paint, not shoes. The connection to the world of shoes and learning about shoes was contrived. This was certainly not a harmful activity, but it wasn't project work. It is unlikely that the activity stimulated children intellectually as much as finding answers to their own questions and problems would have. The thinking that children did was limited to the lower levels of thinking on Bloom's taxonomy. The children are likely to *remember* and *understand* the painting experience, but the concepts to be understood were limited. There may have been some *applying* what they observed about differences in sizes of feet. However, it is unlikely that any deeper analysis of the experience occurred. The creative aspect was limited to what the teacher allowed children to do with their paint-covered feet, which was only to walk across the paper. It is a good example of how a creative teacher will go to great lengths to keep children's attention and engagement.

Contrast foot painting as an intellectual learning experience for children with the experience of figuring out how their own light-up shoes work. This occurred in Barb Gallick's pre-K classroom at Illinois State University Child Care Center. Intrigued by the question, "What makes my shoe light up?" children came up with a way to find the answer. They asked Barb to cut apart an old shoe and then analyzed the parts, which included a battery (see Figure 3.2). They did not understand how a battery worked. She then brought in a flashlight bulb and batteries and placed them in the science area for children to manipulate and experiment. She waited for them to see the similarities between the flashlight and the light-up shoe (see Figure 3.3). Later they compared the parts from the shoe with parts from the flashlight (see Figure 3.4). Eventually they created their own explanation of what makes the light go on in their shoes. Like the foot painting, the children were also likely to *remember* this experience. However, the *understanding* each child had was much more complex. These children learned not just about the parts of a light in a shoe and how it works, but also how a light in a flashlight works. They *analyzed* how the flashlight worked and applied that analysis to the light-up shoe. They created their own theories about what a battery is and does and why the batteries are different shapes for shoes and for flashlights. They also *created* and tested a theory about how stepping on the shoe closes the circuit and makes the shoe light go on.

Barb's role in this engaging learning experience is worth thinking about. Barb observed the high interest of the children and determined that this topic had potential to support intellectual development of the children. She recognized their engagement as an opportunity for higher-level thinking and problem solving. She showed them that they had the power to think deeply about something and come up with their own ideas by letting them plan how they might find the answer to their question, to cut apart the shoe. Because she could cut apart the shoe, and they did not have the strength or skills to do that task, she, as an adult, became a tool for them to use to accomplish that task. Although Barb could have explained to the children how the parts of the shoe worked after they cut it open, she asked them for their ideas. She listened carefully to what they said and assessed their prior knowledge. Each step of the process was determined by her observations of what the children thought and how she might support and encourage them in reaching their goal of understanding how light-up shoes work. She valued their questions and their ideas for finding the answer to their own questions.

This experience began with the children's engagement. Then the progress of the project was in response to that engagement. A topic must engage those children in that classroom at that time. The

Figure 3.2. Barb Gallick cuts apart a light-up shoe under the children's direction.

Figure 3.3. A child experiments with flashlight bulbs and batteries.

Figure 3.4. Aha! A child matches the flashlight battery to the battery in the light-up shoe.

same topic might not engage children in another classroom, or it might not have engaged children in this classroom at a different time of the year.

As discussed in Chapter 1, active engagement drives intellectual growth. If the project topic is one that this particular group of children finds interesting and if the project has many components that can arouse children's curiosity, then they are more likely to take the lead in the investigation. The learning experience then becomes not just about learning concepts inherent within a topic (e.g., the differences between spiders and insects) but about how to organize their own learning and how to satisfy their own curiosity and achieve their own goals. In Dewey's words, children can "learn how to learn." When the project topic is preselected by the teacher and "owned" by the teacher, the project activities are more likely to be teacher planned, prepared, and presented. In some cases, the teacher finds himself "pulling" children through a project. This increases the likelihood that the project results in a learning experience that falls farther to the left on the continuum of child initiation and decision making (refer to Figure 2.5). The project is a teacher-directed thematic unit, and children lose the opportunity to set their own goals and use skills to organize their learning. They are less likely to develop executive function—hill, skill, and will (Moran & Gardner, 2010). Consequently, they are also less likely to experience success and failure resulting from their own efforts or reap the rewards of being persistent and flexible in their thinking. When the topic fails to engage children, they are also less likely to experience how meaningful and handy those reading, writing, and number skills can be in helping them accomplish their own goals. That is, they are less likely to see these academic skills as relevant and useful for their own learning. Furthermore, facilitating a project that does not flow from children's interest can become arduous for the teacher.

Finding an engaging topic that will be meaningful for a specific classroom of children can be a challenge. This process can be made easier if the teacher takes time in Phase I to set the stage for deep project work.

SETTING THE STAGE

Create an Intellectual Environment

The atmosphere of the classroom can make a significant difference in the flow of Phase I and especially in the ability of the teacher to identify a topic. The first MBE Science instructional guideline (see Chapter 1 for a list of all the guidelines mentioned in this chapter) focuses on *Learning Environments*. This guideline refers to the importance of creating an atmosphere of intellectual investigation in the classroom. What does an intellectual atmosphere look like? According to Tokuhoma-Espinosa (2010), it is a classroom that has "respectful exchanges between students and the teacher, a class assessment of what students already know, a clear vision of what they need to know to learn the material well, and the design of learning activities that are student-centered and dynamic" (p. 115). In an early childhood classroom that intellectual environment would include children talking and listening to each other respectfully, the investigation of topics that are meaningful to children, and an overall plan on the part of the teacher that includes assessing and recording children's prior knowledge about a topic. All of this is consistent with classrooms where deep project work occurs.

In a good learning environment for young children—prekindergarten to early elementary—it is especially important to have signals and routines that alert children to ways to behave and interact. There are many times during the day when the teacher will need children to pay close attention to what she is doing and showing. This requires children to be facing the teacher, looking at the item or the teacher's face, listening to what is said, and directing most of the comments to the teacher. This occurs during formal instruction, for example, when the teacher is reading to children or demonstrating a skill. A big task for very young children when they first come to school is learning how to respond appropriately in these instructional situations. Children learn to take turns talking, to stay within their space, to answer teacher questions, and in many cases, to raise their hand to be recognized before talking. These are school skills that are valuable to learn.

However, deep project work often requires children to be more involved with other children, not only participating in the verbal discussion, but also in determining the direction of the discussion. In project discussions, instead of raising their hands and waiting to be recognized, the children respond to one another's questions and comments, challenge others' ideas, and respond spontaneously to more subtle signals to talk such as pauses in the conversation. These are conversation skills that children can learn and practice in project work. During these conversations the teacher encourages children to share their thoughts and ideas freely, to listen and to look not just at the teacher but at other children who are talking.

Both of these types of verbal interaction, teacher-to-child and child-to-child, occur in project work. However, young children often have difficulty determining which interactions are appropriate. There are several strategies that teachers may find support the development of children's ability to contribute to conversations. These strategies include explaining, setting expectations, modeling, adjusting group size, and considering arrangement and location.

Explaining. Children are more likely to respond appropriately if the teacher explains differences in expectations in ways that children can understand. "Pay attention" has little meaning to young children. Asking children to "Put your eyes up here" or "I need to see your eyes looking at me" is understandable to the very young. We need everyone to "close their lips so everyone's ears can hear the story" is concrete. It communicates specifically what the child can do and also provides a clear explanation of why the behavior is desired.

Setting Expectations. This is especially helpful in project work when you have an expert coming to your classroom or when you are preparing for a field site visit. The teacher can explain to the children what the experience will be like. Knowing where they will sit, what the expert might show or share, and how and when they might ask a question will relieve anxieties for very young children and provide an anticipation of engagement. If the

experience is similar to a previous experience, reminding children of that experience may be helpful: "Remember when Mr. Johnson showed us his snake and we all sat on the carpet so we could see? Tomorrow Mrs. Gonzales is going to show us how she uses her sewing machine and answer your questions. We can sit on the rug and listen and look with our eyes just like we did for Mr. Johnson." This enables young children to focus on their questions and the topic.

Modeling. The teacher can listen carefully and assume a position similar to what is desired of the children. Sitting on the floor with the children (and near to those who have the most difficulty focusing) is much more effective than standing over the children to monitor behavior. The teacher can also model responding to other children's comments and questions. A mistake that some teachers make in both large- and small-group discussions is to repeat to the other children what each child has said. In a mistaken attempt to assist the child in getting his message heard, the teacher becomes a translator for the children. This can develop in children a habitual response of waiting for the teacher to repeat before attending to the other children's comments. The teacher can model listening behavior by looking at the child and being attentive. If someone doesn't hear the comment, the teacher can ask the child to repeat what was said. The teacher can also model asking questions.

Adjusting Group Size. There are many opportunities for group gatherings in deep project work. Meeting in groups is encouraged in project work because it builds that sense of community and contributes to that "orchestrated immersion" discussed in MBE Science Instructional Guideline 7. Teachers may find that these experiences are more successful for young children if the size of the group matches the purpose of the gathering. When books are shared, group reports are given, or the group needs to be brought up-to-date on aspects of the project work, a more formal arrangement of the whole group seated facing the teacher or presenter may work best. When a conversation is needed, when the teacher wants all children to have an opportunity to share ideas or discuss problems to be solved, small groups work better. Each child in a small group is more likely to participate in these less formal conversations and to listen and respond to others.

Considering Arrangement and Location. Where and how groups are arranged provide a signal to children regarding expectations for their participation. When children are in a large group that is facing the teacher or the front of the gathering area, theater style, children are encouraged to focus on and listen to whoever is in the front position (see Figure 3.5). When children are seated in a small group and form a circle, then each child can see the faces of everyone including the teacher who also sits in the circle (see Figure 3.6). This arrangement encourages children to listen more to one another, to talk more to the other children, and to direct fewer comments to the teacher only. Location within the room can also encourage children to participate in small-group discussions. A project discussion group can meet in another area of the room, rather than in the same location in which more formal teacher-led activities such as big book reading occurs. Block areas or reading nooks in early childhood classrooms can be used for small groups. Even a round table with chairs will work well, especially with primary children. The teacher can also highlight the change in the way interaction will take place during project discussions by explaining, "When we come here to have a conversation about our project work, everyone can talk. We don't have to raise our hands before we talk. We just take turns."

Summing Up. Taking the time to set the stage by teaching children how to interact within groups in a meaningful way is time well spent. There is a social nature to effective learning experiences (MBE Science Instructional Guideline 5). Learning is enhanced when teachers provide opportunities for social interaction. Projects are a perfect opportunity for a teacher to structure learning experiences to encourage interaction and active exchanges of perceptions and information. When a possible topic is first identified is a good time for

Figure 3.5. Pam Scranton arranges children in a group facing her for some learning experiences, such as reading a big book.

Figure 3.6. During project discussions, such as this one about flashlights, Pam has children sit in a small group facing each other so they can focus on listening and talking to one another.

the teacher to establish the routine of these meaningful small- and large-group discussions. The children's ability to listen and talk to others in a meaningful way is a skill that will deepen project work throughout the investigation phase and on into the culminating phase as children decide how to share what they have learned. These discussions also provide an opportunity for teachers to work on metacognition (MBE Science Instructional Guideline 9). Meeting regularly to discuss the project process provides that critical time for reflection and for children to "think about their own thinking." By age 3, most children have some awareness of their own thinking processes and distinguish between thinking about something and simply perceiving (Flavell, Green, & Flavell, 1995). As children reflect on their own interest and their unique thoughts about the topic, they not only practice the vocabulary related to the project topic but also develop words to describe what they are feeling and thinking. This also facilitates children's grasp of new concepts and can maximize memory consolidation (MBE Science Instructional Guideline 3).

All of these strategies are designed to create that atmosphere of intellectual investigation in which even very young children can contribute their thoughts and ideas and respond to one another respectfully. When this occurs, the teacher can more easily assess the children's interest and background knowledge on the topic. Of course, none of these group experiences replaces the ongoing one-to-one conversations teachers have with children or the spontaneous discussions that happen with one or two children during daily activities.

Assess Sense and Meaning of a Topic

One of the purposes of discussing topics in both individual conversations and large-group meetings is to assess if the topic makes sense and has meaning for the children in the classroom (MBE Science Instructional Guideline 2). For a topic to make sense and have meaning to young children, it must have a strong connection to the children's lives, to the culturally based neural network already established. The brain learns new information by connecting it to information that is already familiar to the child. Skills are learned when the use of those skills makes sense to children as something that can be used in their lives, either now or in the future. To determine how a topic might connect to children's lives, the teacher must know a lot about the children and their families. Teachers can learn this by listening to their play events and paying attention to conversations they have with other children about what they do with their families on weekends and how the family spends time outside of the center or school. Many excellent project topics have been identified by teachers as they converse with children over snacks or meals and other informal times.

For example, one group of children noticed construction equipment on a field near their school. During snack time that morning the children become animated talking about what they saw and about other places they had seen construction equipment. Construction equipment became a possible topic for a project.

As seen in Phase I of the flow chart (refer to Figure 3.1), not all topics emerge from the children; they can be teacher initiated. Sometimes a teacher will foresee an opportunity for a topic to engage children. For example, in the Construction Equipment Project the teacher learned that there would be a construction site near the school and then walked the children to the site to observe. During the observation, the children became very interested in the different pieces of construction equipment and asked many questions. Both of these experiences—informal observation of children's interest and a teacher-planned encounter—are ways that a deep project investigation can start.

An important next step is for the teacher to collect and document prior knowledge about a topic by using one or more of the following strategies:

- Have a free-form discussion about the topic, asking for stories of the children.
- Provide opportunities for children to draw or paint what they know about the topic. Have children tell about their work. Collect and analyze.
- Place items in the classroom that will stimulate play related to the topic and observe the children's play.
- Create a project web of what the children know.
- Create smaller webs of different aspects of the topic to define what is the most interesting to children.
- Create a list of words children use that are related to the topic to determine background knowledge.

In addition to providing the teacher with an understanding of children's prior knowledge, these strategies also refresh and extend children's memory (MBE Science Instructional Guideline 3) and provide a metacognitive experience for children (MBE Science Instructional Guideline 9). Taking the time for reflection and to "think about their own thinking" about the topic will enable them to grasp new concepts easier.

Based on what the teacher learned about children's prior knowledge, he may arrange focusing events to build background knowledge on a topic and to make sure that all children have enough information and connection with the topic for it to be engaging for the whole class. Children's background knowledge of the topic can be built with books, media, storytelling, or exploration of artifacts so that all children have a network of knowledge on which to connect.

Determine Children's Interest

During and after the focusing activities and common experiences, the teacher continues to evaluate the topic's worthiness for project work. She gathers evidence and documentation regarding whether or not the topic makes sense and is meaningful to the children and whether or not it meets the other criteria for selection of a topic. During this time the teacher is assessing which particular aspects of the topic most engage the children and which children are engaged by which aspect of the topic. For example, on a topic on shoes, some children may be very interested in the structure of a shoe, how it is made, and the names of the parts. Other children may not be interested in the shoe itself but are very interested in the business of shoes, especially the selling and buying of shoes. One of the hallmarks of deep project work is that there are a variety of opportunities for children to connect with the project topic, that "orchestrated immersion" of MBE Science Instructional Guideline 7. As the teacher observes and notes level of engagement, the teacher can narrow the topic to maximize children's emotional involvement and engagement and can also plan learning experiences so that there is something in the topic that engages each child.

Because the ability to determine the level of engagement is important in this phase, it might be helpful to clarify what engagement looks like in a preschool or early primary classroom. Most teachers can tell if children are engaged in the learning experiences they are providing. However, I have found that some teachers, and especially those new to teaching, may be unaware or miss the cues of engagement in young children. Some of the behaviors that indicate that children are actively thinking and involved in a learning experience are the following:

- Focusing their eyes on the artifact or material
- Participating with enthusiasm in a conversation by looking at the person speaking
- Asking and answering questions
- Stating what they see ("Look how big his eyes are!")
- Moving close so they can see artifacts or participate in a topic-related activity
- Asking for a turn to interact (such as touching the turtle)
- Sitting or standing very still rather than randomly moving about or becoming easily sidetracked with other things (such as the lint on the rug)
- Showing expressions of joy, excitement, puzzlement, or other emotions
- Telling about their own personal experiences
- Spending an unusually long time involved in topic-related activities

Of course, determining the level of engagement of children requires that the teacher take the time to observe and listen closely to the children. In Figure 3.7 Michelle is listening carefully to a child's observations about differences between the seeds he has selected and placed in his hand and the ones on the table. Another child becomes so engaged in this exploration that he forgets the rules and climbs on the table for a closer look. Both of these children are exhibiting engagement behaviors. By looking for these types of behaviors, the teacher can determine what is the most interesting to children and what particular aspects of the topic are engaging to specific children. These observations and the children's questions enable the teacher to plan next steps.

Figure 3.7. Children in the Seed Store Project examine seeds gathered during a walk in the woods. What behaviors indicate engagement?

Recognize Distance from Self

As pointed out earlier, topics that relate to the child's current life experiences create more opportunities for the child to connect new knowledge and concepts with existing knowledge so new concepts are easier to learn (MBE Science Instructional Guideline 2). One way to deepen project work, then, is to choose topics with the highest probability of engagement for your group and/or to increase the relevance of the project topic to your group. The probability of a topic engaging children in a specific classroom is difficult to predict. There are, however, some general guidelines that a teacher can use. In *Young Investigators*, Helm and Katz (2011) utilized the circular diagram by Bess-Gene Holt (1989) and Holt's concept of Distance from Self. The premise of the diagram is that the more the learning experience is connected to the children's own immediate daily reality—to their own concept of self—the more successful it will be. Since I first introduced the idea of applying Holt's diagram to assist in project selection, reviews of deep project work and discussions about topic selection have provided additional insight into how this diagram is helpful to teachers. For that reason, in Figure 3.8, I have added three numbered circles to indicate projects more likely to deeply engage children and result in deep project work at certain levels of development.

1. The first circle encompasses topics encountered in the world of the *toddler*. These include what happens in immediate time (now), what is in the toddler's own space and shelter (what is in her house), things used to care for the toddler, food the toddler eats, and what the toddler recognizes will keep her warm. Some project topics that have been especially successful with toddlers have included hair care, toddler toys, boxes, and things they see on daily walks such as a tree, car, or fire hydrant, as well as objects used for their care such as car seats.

2. The second circle (which also encompasses the topics in Circle 1) includes topics in the immediate world of the *preschooler*. Some project topics that have resulted in deep projects are their toys, their relatives, their own culture, buildings and businesses around them, equipment that they see used, their neighbors, adults in their school, plants observed in their world, their playground, local wildlife, pets, and pests.

3. The third circle (which includes everything in Circles 1 and 2) shows topics in the immediate world of the *kindergartner* and *1st-grader*. Project topics that have resulted in deep project work with kindergartners and beginning primary-age children include farms, ponds, and animal habitats. Children of this age are also interested in changes in heat, sound, air, and light. Although they are often interested in stories of the past, it is difficult for them to do independent investigation and to understand when these events occurred. All the topics listed above for Circle 2 are still good project topics for this age group.

Deep project work requires a high level of children's engagement and the ability of the children to authentically direct their own learning. To be able to do this, children must have enough familiarity and interest in the topic to enable them to think about what they know and what they want to know so they can set their own goals. If the children's experience with a topic is limited to what the teacher has told them, what they have read in a

Figure 3.8. Distance from Self Diagram

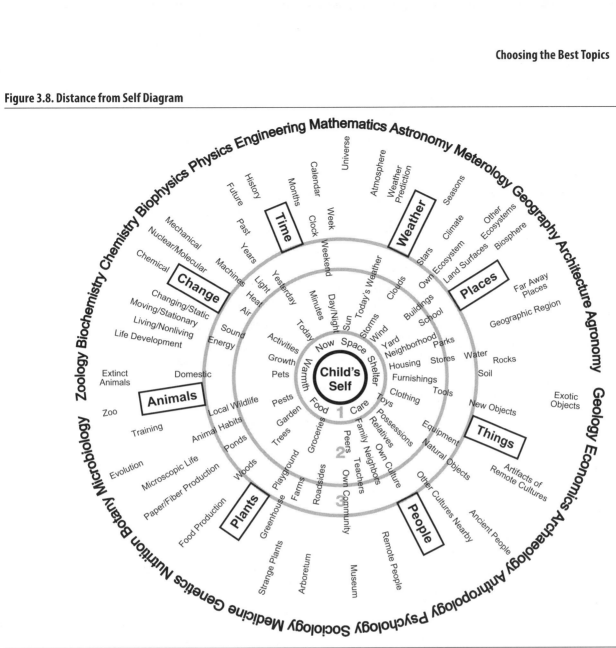

book or seen on a video, their background knowledge is limited. Young children are less likely to see how a topic integrates with other experiences they have had, and they are less likely to become truly engaged. For example, if children have not seen the ocean or visited a beach, then they are limited to the resources that the teacher has provided about the beach. Books, videos, and descriptions (such as the teacher's description of her visit to the ocean) are secondhand experiences that do not provide opportunities for the children to directly observe and experience. These secondhand experiences lack the sensory richness necessary for deep engagement. Their interest and curiosity will be limited to those concepts that the teacher has selected to share with

the children. The immensity of the ocean, the relationship between the sand and waves, and the complexity of the beach environment with all the plants and animals are most likely missing from children's understanding when it is based solely on the resources the teacher is able to bring into the classroom. The topic of oceans for children in the Midwest could be classified as a "far away place" and is located in the outer circle in the Distance from Self diagram (Figure 3.8). Contrast that with the topic of the pond in a park near the children's school or center. On the diagram the neighborhood pond would be located in Circle 2, "neighborhood." The neighborhood pond can be observed and experienced firsthand.

Topics that are in the outer circle of the Distance from Self diagram require the ability to use secondary sources of investigation such as the Internet, journals written by others, or diagrams by adults. These require enough proficiency in academic skills such as reading with comprehension before they can be used for independent, student-directed research. This vicarious learning through the interpretation of others when it is used as the only learning experience is not as effective with young children and doesn't contribute to their intellectual development as much as hands-on, child-directed learning. However, when these secondhand experiences (books, Internet sites, and so on) accompany hands-on, child-directed investigations as in project work, they then become meaningful sources and enable children to see the value of academic skills such as reading and writing.

Those topics in the outer circle also extend outside of the time range that young children understand. For example, Costa Rican rain forests and endangered species require the understanding of both time (years and history) and distance (faraway places, regions, and exotic objects). A better topic for prekindergarten children would be related to what is in their immediate environment, current (not historical), and within their own experiences. The use of the Distance from Self diagram is especially helpful in determining topics for deep, extended investigations. This does not mean that teachers should refrain from reading books, sharing their experiences, or using electronic resources about topics not in the immediate world of children. These can be used in other parts of the curriculum or other times in the day and will build vocabulary and develop background knowledge. However, when the topic matches the Distance from Self of the children, deep child-directed investigations are more likely to occur.

Evaluate with Topic Guidelines

There are a number of other considerations in choosing a project topic besides whether or not the topic makes sense and has meaning for the children in a particular classroom. Katz and Chard (2000) provide topic-selection guidelines for planning projects for children of any age.

In *Young Investigators* (Helm & Katz, 2011, Chapter 2), general guidelines are also provided for topics that work especially well with children who are not yet proficient in reading and writing. In addition, considerations come from Dewey (described in Chapter 2) and from MBE Science (see Chapter 1). This is a lengthy list; however, the selection of an appropriate topic is often the key to building a deep project experience for young children. Below is a summary of some of the major points from all of these sources that teachers have found helpful. The topic will probably work well if the teacher can answer yes to most of these questions:

- Is the topic anchored in children's own experiences, and does it help them understand and appreciate their own world?
- Does the topic add enough value to the children's experience to justify the educational time devoted to the topic?
- Are there items and processes within the topic that encourage children to examine things closely and to observe with accuracy?
- Does the topic provide opportunities for children to use a variety of skills during investigation?
- Are there experiences related to the topic that would enable children to develop those dispositions outlined in Chapter 2 (Katz, 1993)?
- Does the topic provide opportunities for children to represent what they have learned in a variety of ways and to develop skills in representation?
- Is this a topic that is more concrete than abstract?
- Is there an abundance of firsthand, direct experiences and real objects that young investigators can manipulate?
- Can children do their own research with minimal assistance from adults? Can it be researched without relying only on secondary sources like books, the Internet, or videos?
- Are there authentic artifacts and processes that children can study firsthand and not be

dependent on adult's models, interpretations, photos, drawings, and other secondary source material to learn about the topic?

- Does the topic have related field sites nearby that can be conveniently visited and even revisited?
- Is the topic culturally relevant to the children and their families?
- Will there be opportunities for children to solve their own problems and do their own higher-level thinking including analyzing, evaluating, and creating?
- Do the children find the topic engaging and interesting?
- Does it further the children's core understanding of curriculum, and does it help children meet age-relevant standards such as the Common Core State Standards?

Of all of these questions, however, the most important for developing really deep project work are the last two criteria: (1) degree of engagement and interest in the topic and (2) the potential for developing children's core understandings of the curriculum.

CONSIDERING CURRICULUM GOALS AND STANDARDS

The project approach is an approach to curriculum. Therefore, curriculum requirements are an important part of the topic selection process. Facilitating projects following the structure of the project approach is one way, but not the only way, to meet curriculum goals. Considering whether or not a topic fits into the context of required curriculum or will contribute to meeting standards, such as the Common Core State Standards, is an important component of topic selection.

Common Core State Standards

Most public school programs in the United States are in the process of implementing the Common Core State Standards. As noted in Chapter 1, this new set of academic standards for kindergarten

through high school attempts to provide a consistent, clear understanding of what students are expected to learn, so teachers and parents know what they need to do to help them. One of the purposes of the CCSS is to provide standards that are relevant to the real world. This means that children will do better if their education is connected to the real world. The variations of project learning, as described in Chapter 2, are becoming a focus of interest because project work can assist teachers in meeting the 21st-century goals. I believe the project approach can be very helpful to teachers in kindergarten and the early primary grades because it provides a way to incorporate the CCSS in a developmentally appropriate way. The structure of the phases, the planning process described in Chapter 4, and the strategies for questions and provocations in Chapters 5 and 7 can enable teachers to both meet standards and provide engaged learning experiences to the children in their classroom.

Appendix C provides a summary of the English language arts CCSS. The chart presents which standards naturally occur in the project-approach process and those that can be integrated with a little extra planning and effort. Appendix D provides the same type of chart for mathematics. These are the only two content areas of CCSS that apply to kindergarten and primary grades at this time. The Illinois Early Learning and Development Standards, presented in the next section as an example of state standards, were written to align with the CCSS.

Required Curriculum and Potential Topics

Most publicly funded pre-K to grade 2 programs have some form of required curriculum or standards. Terminology for these varies from program to program and from state to state. Standards that address specific skills such as those needed for problem solving, reasoning, and communicating. These *skill standards* relate to what the children are learning how to do and include strategies that they can apply widely to a variety of situations to solve problems. Standards that list specific content that students should learn at each grade level are called *content standards*. They define the knowledge within each discipline. These include concepts unique to the discipline, such as the concept of a life cycle. A common standard for this age level is "understanding that living things grow and change." These content standards refer to specific knowledge that a child should know and provide an order and an understanding of the structure of that knowledge area. Sometimes there are separate lists of content standards and skill standards (e.g., science knowledge and science skills). More often at this age level these are combined under one set of science standards.

Skill standards. In preschool through the early years of elementary school (K–2) a major focus is the learning of reading, writing, and numeracy skills. As Dewey indicates, these skills are an essential component of learning how to learn. Understanding the value of these skills and learning how to apply them is a component of the investigation process and deep project work. Opportunities to develop social–emotional skills and using the arts for expression are also prominent skills developed in project work. When observing deeply engaging and effective applications of the project approach in pre-K to grade 2 classrooms, one sees a wealth of examples of children's reading, drawing, writing, data gathering, counting, and representations as part of their project work. Learning and applying these skills permeates the project process. Documentation of skill goals and standards achieved in these areas appear in almost all deep project work regardless of the content of the topic. That is, skill-oriented benchmarks can be achieved in project work whether the topic is a science topic such as "seeds" or a social studies topic such as the "drive-up bank." Many of these skill standards occur naturally through the process of following the project approach structure (e.g., in the process of interviewing experts). In addition, some required curriculum standards are easily incorporated into the project process when the teacher provides additional opportunities to achieve them (e.g., predicting what an expert might say or what an animal might eat, then recording the predictions and what they found out).

I recommend that teachers review and analyze their standards and benchmarks so they understand how these are structured, how they might most easily be integrated into project work, and how they might be helpful in making decisions about topic selection. For example, the Illinois Early Learning and Development Standards (IELDS; llinois State Board of Education, 2013) provide a comprehensive resource of reasonable expectations for the development of children in the preschool years (ages 3 to 5) for all teachers across the state of Illinois. The IELDS parallel content in the Illinois State Goals for Learning and align with the Illinois Kindergarten Standards and the Common Core State Standards for Kindergarten. All domains or areas of development are included so the focus is on the whole child. Many of these standards are achieved naturally through the project approach process. Figure 3.9 lists those standards that are skill oriented. These are marked with a check mark (✓) when the standard naturally occurs in the process of doing a project. Standards that can be easily included in project work with some extra planning are marked with a plus sign (+). These standards can apply to almost any topic.

Often guidelines for standards include additional information that is helpful for teacher planning. For example, in the IELDS, the standards are broad, but they are accompanied by benchmarks that provide guidance for the specific age level. Preschool benchmarks provide teachers with specific ways that preschool children demonstrate those learning standards at the preschool age level. Benchmarks for the preschool Learning Standard 11.A, "Develop beginning skills in the use of science and engineering practices, such as observing, asking questions, solving problems, and drawing conclusions," include the following:

- Express wonder and curiosity about their world by asking questions, solving problems, and designing things. (11.A.ECa).
- Develop and use models to represent their ideas, observations, and explanations through approaches such as drawing, building, or modeling with clay. (11.A.ECb).
- Plan and carry out simple investigations. (11.A.ECc).

Figure 3.9. Skill-Oriented Standards from the Illinois Early Learning and Development Standards

> ✓ occurs naturally in project approach process
> + can be easily included in project work

LANGUAGE ARTS

✓ 1.A Demonstrate understanding through age-appropriate responses.

✓ 1.B Communicate effectively using language appropriate to the situation and audience.

✓ 1.C Use language to convey information and ideas.

+ 1.D Speak using conventions of Standard English.

✓ 1.E Use increasingly complex phrases, sentences, and vocabulary.

✓ 2.A Demonstrate interest in stories and books.

+ 2.B Recognize key ideas and details in stories.

✓ 2.C Recognize concepts of books.

✓ 2.D Establish personal connections with books.

✓ 3.A Recognize key ideas and details in nonfiction text.

+ 3.B Recognize features of nonfiction books.

+ 4.A Demonstrate understanding of the organization and basic features of print.

+ 4.B Demonstrate an emerging knowledge and understanding of the alphabet.

+ 4.C Demonstrate an emerging understanding of spoken words, syllables, and sounds (phonemes).

+ 4.D Demonstrate emergent phonics and word-analysis skills.

✓ 5.A Demonstrate growing interest and abilities in writing .

✓ 5.B Use writing to represent ideas and information.

✓ 5.C Use writing to research and share knowledge.

MATHEMATICS

✓ 6.A Demonstrate beginning understanding of numbers, number names, and numerals.

+ 6.B Add and subtract to create new numbers and begin to construct sets.

✓ 6.C Begin to make reasonable estimates of numbers.

✓ 6.D Compare quantities using appropriate vocabulary terms.

+ 7.A Measure objects and quantities using direct comparison methods and nonstandard units.

+ 7.B Begin to make estimates of measurements.

+ 7.C Explore tools used for measurement.

✓ 8.A Explore objects and patterns.

+ 8.B Describe and document patterns using symbols.

+ 9.A Recognize, name, and match common shapes.

+ 9.B Demonstrate understanding of location and ordinal position, using appropriate vocabulary.

✓ 10.A Generate questions and processes for answering them.

✓ 10.B Organize and describe data and information.

+ 10.C Determine, describe, and apply the probabilities of events.

SCIENCE

✓ 11.A Develop beginning skills in the use of science and engineering practices, such as observing, asking questions, solving problems, and drawing conclusions.

✓ 12.C Explore the physical properties of objects.

✓ 13.A Understand rules to follow when investigating and exploring.

✓ 13.B Use tools and technology to assist with science and engineering investigations.

SOCIAL STUDIES

✓ 14.C Understand ways groups make choices and decisions.

✓ 14.D Understand the role that individuals can play in a group or community.

+ 15.B Explore issues of limited resources in the early childhood environment and world.

✓ 16.A Explore his or her self and personal history.

PHYSICAL DEVELOPMENT AND HEALTH

✓ 19.C Demonstrate knowledge of rules and safety during activity.

THE ARTS

✓ 25.A Investigate, begin to appreciate, and participate in the arts.

✓ 25.B Display an awareness of some distinct characteristics of the arts.

✓ 26.A Understand processes, traditional tools, and modern technologies used in the arts.

✓ 26.B Understand ways to express meaning through the arts.

ENGLISH LANGUAGE LEARNER HOME LANGUAGE DEVELOPMENT

✓ 28.A Use the home language at age-appropriate levels for a variety of social and academic purposes.

✓ 29.A Use the home language to attain benchmarks across all the learning areas and to build upon and develop transferable language and literacy skills.

SOCIAL/EMOTIONAL DEVELOPMENT

✓ 30.A Identify and manage one's emotions and behavior.

+ 30.B Recognize own uniqueness and personal qualities.

✓ 30.C Demonstrate skills related to successful personal and school outcomes.

✓ 31.A Develop positive relationships with peers and adults.

✓ 31.B Use communication and social skills to interact effectively with others.

✓ 31.C Demonstrate an ability to prevent, manage, and resolve interpersonal conflicts in constructive ways.

✓ 32.A Begin to consider ethical, safety, and societal factors in making decisions.

✓ 32.B Apply decision-making skills to deal responsibly with daily academic and social situations.

+ 32.C Contribute to the well-being of one's school and community.

- Collect, describe, compare, and record information from observations and investigations. (11.A.ECd)
- Use mathematical and computational thinking. (11.A.ECe)
- Make meaning from experience and information by describing, talking, and thinking about what happened during an investigation. (11.A.ECf)
- Generate explanations and communicate ideas and/or conclusions about their investigations. (11.A.ECg)

When benchmarks are provided the teacher can think ahead about how a project topic might evolve.

Content Standards. However, project work is not just about learning and applying skills; it is also about building background knowledge and meeting content goals. These *content standards* pertain to knowledge and understanding of a specific content area, such as science or social studies. These content standards are good starting points in the search for a topic. Again, the benchmarks that accompany these standards provide assistance in project topic selection because they designate broad topics of study and can connect to many potential topics. These examples are again from the IELDS (llinois State Board of Education, 2013)

Standard: Understand that living things grow and change. (12A)
Benchmarks: Observe, investigate, describe, and categorize living things; show an awareness of changes that occur in oneself and the environment. (12A.ECa)

Standard: Understand that living things rely on the environment and/or others to live and grow. (12B)
Benchmarks: Describe and compare basic needs of living things; show respect for living things. (12B.ECa)

A deep investigation of almost any living and growing thing that children found to be of deep interest (e.g., turtles, dogs, corn, and fish) or their

habitats (e.g., the pond, the lake, the garden) would enable a teacher to meet these standards. The Social Studies standards and benchmarks from IELDS (llinois State Board of Education, 2013) also provide promising topics:

Standard: Explore roles in the economic system and workforce. (15A)
Benchmarks: Describe some common jobs and what is needed to perform those jobs (15A.ECa); discuss why people work. (15A.ECb)

Standard: Explore concepts about trade as an exchange of goods or services. (15D)
Benchmarks: Begin to understand the use of trade or money to obtain goods and services. (15D.ECa)

Standard: Explore environments and where people live. (17A)
Benchmarks: Locate objects and places in familiar environments (17A. ECa); express beginning geographic thinking. (17A.ECb)

A deep investigation of most businesses or jobs for which children show interest (e.g., businesses such as a pizza restaurant or a bank, jobs such as veterinarian) would enable the teacher to provide experiences within these prescribed curriculum areas. Another content area that provides rich potential for project work is the arts. These arts standards and benchmarks are from IELDS (llinois State Board of Education, 2013):

Standard: Investigate, begin to appreciate, and participate in the arts. (25A)
Benchmarks:
- Movement and Dance: Build awareness of, explore, and participate in dance and creative movement activities. (25A.ECa)
- Drama: Begin to appreciate and participate in dramatic activities. (25A.ECb)
- Music: Begin to appreciate and participate in music activities. (25A. ECc)
- Visual Arts: Investigate and participate in activities using visual arts materials. (25A.ECd)

Studies of specific types of dance, drama, music, or visual art have resulted in some deep project work including the development of an art museum, dance productions, and musical instruments.

Most of the deep project work that I have observed in pre-K to grade 2 classrooms has focused on the content areas of science, social studies, or the arts with significant integration of the language arts skills and mathematical thinking experiences.

Integrated Topics

The segregation of skills and content is helpful in searching for topics within curriculum standards; however, this separation is more within adult minds than within the minds of children. As they begin to master the basic skills of reading, writing, and numeracy, then the variety of potential topics for deep project work increases. This can also be seen in the standards for more advanced age levels. Skills and content become more blended within the curriculum as children's skills increase, as their background knowledge increases, and as they develop greater ability to think symbolically. This often occurs by about 3rd grade when they are less dependent on concrete experiences and have developed a sense of time, and their world has widened.

Even in pre-K to grade 2 classrooms, the best topics cross many curriculum areas and integrate both content standards and skills.

ADDRESSING COMMON ISSUES IN TOPIC SELECTION

Holt's Distance from Self diagram (refer to Figure 3.8), the level of engagement of the children, and curriculum requirements can provide a framework that teachers can rely on for choosing a project topic with deep potential. However, there are also several points in the topic identification process about which teachers usually have questions.

Narrowing of a Topic

A consideration of many teachers striving for deep project work is how far to go in narrowing the topic (e.g., from restaurants to pizza restaurants to Tony's Pizza Parlor on Fifth Avenue). The answer, as in much project work, is, "It depends." It depends on the level of engagement of the children and the goals for this particular group of children. Generally, broad topics tend to result in learning and practicing fewer new words. For example, in a broad project topic such as restaurants, children may brainstorm different kinds of restaurants that they know about such as pizza restaurants, Chinese restaurants, take-out restaurants, and so on. In a project focusing on all these restaurants they might compare what is served, how the restaurants differ in physical layout, and even menu differences. They tend to talk about and describe these restaurants using words they already know and are less likely to encounter new specific words. They are more likely to visit or interview experts from several different restaurants, and conversation will tend to be focused on differences. The concepts encountered tend to be symbolic and less concrete. The discussions are often limited to one content area, such as social studies. The more abstract the topic, the less likely it is to engage children and provide opportunities for successful investigation for all, rather than just a few, children (orchestrated immersion, MBE Science Instructional Guideline 7).

When the topic narrows to a specific type of restaurant, such as a pizza restaurant, the experience becomes rich with concrete things (artifacts) to learn about. The discussion is likely to be more about things that can be investigated firsthand, that can be touched, manipulated, and used for play. In an investigation of a pizza restaurant, children will want to know about making, selling, and delivering pizzas. They will learn about different types of pizza and the ingredients, the different sizes and how they are measured, the equipment needed to produce pizzas, and how they are placed in and removed from the oven. The topic may narrow even further. Topics that might emerge in this narrowing process could include Tony's Pizza Parlor on Fifth Avenue, the production of pizza at Tony's, where the pizza ovens are located, where Tony orders and stores supplies, or how he delivers his pizza. As children visit and interview experts, more detailed questions are asked, and this results in new vocabulary, specifically words for concrete things, which are then incorporated into play experiences where they are practiced daily, leading to retention. Quite simply, Tony's Pizza on Fifth Avenue is more engaging to the children.

Project topics can also become too narrow. For example, if the topic narrows not just to Tony's Pizza but to the pizza only, this reduces the vocabulary to be learned (such as supplier, inventory), the curriculum concepts encountered (such as the idea of buying and selling), and the opportunity to integrate curriculum goals across content areas (such as menu making, advertising campaigns).

There are some topics that start with the children narrowly focused on a project topic, such as the Map Project, which began in Lora Taylor's preschool classroom when a map blew into the playground. This project expanded beyond the map to investigating how to find one's way. There is, of course, no definitive answer to how much one should narrow or broaden a topic. There are, however, some rules of thumb that teachers have found helpful:

1. Begin by evaluating the degree of engagement children have with the topic and with specific components of the topic. Take notes and review conversations.
2. How many children are engaged in the topic? Will broadening or narrowing the topic increase the number of children who find a way to be engaged?

3. How many curriculum goals can be authentically integrated into the narrower topic? How many in the larger topic?
4. What field sites and expert visitors are available? Which of these will be the most meaningful to children?

How Much Direction Is Too Much?

Teachers often ask how much direction in project selection is too much. Again this is difficult to answer because classrooms vary so much in the children's current skills, experience in project work, and the academic and social–emotional needs. A teacher may provide a great deal of input on a topic that occurs early in the school year, whereas a project that occurs the following spring may be much more child directed. However, it is important to remember that, according to John Dewey, teachers can direct the child's activities leading up to goals. The project approach is an approach to curriculum and the achievement of curriculum goals. The teacher is responsible for the effectiveness of learning experiences in her classroom, and the topic selected can be a major determinant of the likelihood of meeting curriculum goals. As long as the teacher remembers to also adhere to the MBE Science instructional guidelines—especially those referring to an intellectual environment (1), sense and meaning (2), orchestrated immersion (7), and active processes (8)—then she will most likely contribute not just to the knowledge and skills of the children but also to the development of their mind and brain capacity.

CHAPTER 4

Refining the Planning Process

Deep project work doesn't happen by accident. Neither does incorporation of curriculum goals or achievement of standards, such as the CCSS. I have concluded from survey results and conversations during training events that many teachers still find the integration of curriculum goals to be challenging. In most project classrooms teachers do an excellent job of recognizing when curriculum goals occur naturally in project work. They often document and spotlight these goals in displays and communications to parents and administrators. Curriculum goals are recognized in the process of organizing documentation or culminating the project. Sometimes a teacher will think about integrating a goal while teaching on the fly during the process of project work. These are important times to think about curriculum goals and can be quite effective. However, the teacher can increase the likelihood that curriculum goals will be achieved by careful, complete planning. In the Deepening Project Work Survey, 92% of the teachers said that they had curriculum goals and/or standards that they were required to teach. However, less than 45% said that they had planned in advance how they might incorporate goals into their projects, and 25% said they did not use an anticipatory planning web for planning.

In observing project work, I have found that when I see a classroom involved in engaging and thought-provoking project work, I usually find written evidence that careful planning occurred before the project began. In projects that are extremely rich with opportunities for children to learn desired (or in many cases required) knowledge, skills, and dispositions, teachers do extensive planning work and spend considerable time thinking about curriculum goals. That means they take the time to review the standards that apply to their age level, such as the Common Core State Standards, and use them as a central component of their planning process. "Hope is not a strategy" can be properly applied to curriculum integration in project work.

TEACHER AS PLANNER

As we learned from John Dewey in Chapter 2, teachers have to plan and prepare for good educational experiences. Although he emphasized that the role of the teacher in the project approach is to facilitate and guide the project process, she is still an educational leader. A contemporary perspective on the need for a teacher to be proactive comes from the National Research Council's recommendations on early childhood pedagogy:

> Children need opportunities to initiate activities and follow their interests, but teachers are not passive during these initiated and directed activities. Similarly children should be actively engaged and responsive during teacher-initiated and directed activities. Good teachers help support the child's learning in both types of activities. They also recognize that children learn from each other and from interactions with the physical environment. (Bowman, Donovan, & Burns, 2000, p. 11)

In project work, the teacher has an opportunity to provide learning experiences that are both child initiated and directed and teacher initiated and directed, in addition to ample opportunities for children to work together. These experiences, however, are less likely to occur without careful planning and preparation by the teacher. Another contemporary perspective on teacher planning comes from the literature on intentional teaching:

> Intentional teaching means teachers act with specific outcomes or goals in mind for children's development and learning. Teachers must know when to use a given strategy to accommodate the different ways that individual children learn and the specific content they are learning. (Epstein, 2007, p. 1)

During the process of project work it is essential that the teacher be intentional, that he "intentionally and consciously" observe and listen to children carefully to determine the direction of the project. However, the teacher who is also intentional about planning for a new topic with specific outcomes and goals for children's learning and development, who intentionally plans his role in project work, is more likely to provide a deep, rich project experience for his children. Intentional planning includes deciding which materials to gather and introduce. It also includes planning initial experiences with the topic so children can build background knowledge, become familiar with initial vocabulary, and learn some initial concepts about the topic. As discussed further in Chapter 5, these initial activities provide a critical knowledge base for the young investigators to draw on and are especially important for very young children. These activities, when carefully planned and executed, also provide specific opportunities for the teacher to observe the children's interest in the topic.

An example of how planning and preparation can be helpful can be seen in this hypothetical Shoe Project. The teacher selected the general topic of shoes by carefully thinking about children's informal conversations in the classroom and looking for topics that were close to the children's world, as discussed in the section "Recognize Distance from Self" in Chapter 3. To build common background knowledge about shoes, the teacher introduced shoes into the housekeeping area and spent some of circle time directing children to examine and talk about their shoes. The teacher also anticipated children's interest in the differences between shoes and prepared for this experience by having shoe catalogs and flyers about shoes available. To focus children's attention on the characteristics of their shoes, she also brought a camera so if children's interest was strong, she could be ready to photograph each child's shoes to create a new resource, which she did. The catalogs, flyers, and photographs were placed in the book area after the discussion. As the discussion progressed, she used these resources to reinforce a common vocabulary. She listened carefully to the conversation to see what aspects of the world of shoes were most interesting to the children.

This is an example of well-planned activities in Phase I of the project approach likely to develop into deep project work. This project might narrow to focus on a shoe store, a shoe repair shop, or the making of shoes, or even expand the initial sorting experiences into a deeper exploration of shoe parts and materials. The project will be deeper and more meaningful because the children have developed a common vocabulary for discussions and generation of questions.

Important also to the success of this phase was the teacher's grounding of curriculum decisions in the standards and required curriculum. She knew that Scientific Investigation, Reasoning, and Logic are part of the Standards of Learning (SOL) in her state (Virginia Department of Education, 2010). Specifically, she knew that children in her classroom would need to learn to make observations, separate objects into groups based on similar attributes, compare lengths and mass, and be able to develop questions based upon observation using the five senses.

TYING TOGETHER STANDARDS AND TOPICS

To some teachers who struggle to keep projects vibrant and children involved in their classrooms, the teacher with the hypothetical shoe project might appear either creative or lucky. Most teachers find it easy to think about having a conversation, having children examine or sort shoes, or reading a story about shoes. Incorporating shoes into the housekeeping area is also fairly easy to think of. However, fewer teachers would have thought to bring in shoe catalogs and flyers or to use their cameras to create photos of children's shoes. This happened because the teacher was systematic in her planning and intentionally focused the children on the aspect of the topic she had predicted, based on her observations, would be most likely to engage all children and create conversation. Then she thought beyond conversation to how this interest might mesh with curriculum goals and standards. This is the benefit of anticipatory planning.

Often deep, rich project work can be traced to deep, rich planning. One strategy that has become effective for making this planning happen is the use of the teacher's anticipatory planning web. This process is introduced in *Young Investigators* (Helm & Katz, 2011, pp. 101–102). It is a planning process at the beginning of a project *anticipating* the possibilities for curriculum integration and child interest. This process has been expanded to increase the probability of deep project work and is described in the next section. Teachers who want to deepen their project work should find this process helpful. However, there are two prerequisites to enable intentional planning: (1) Teachers have to have crystal-clear understanding of the knowledge, skills, and dispositions that they are supposed to teach; and (2) teachers have to have a clear understanding of the interests and daily experiences of their children.

Understanding of Curriculum and Standards

A teacher can do a simple self-check of his knowledge about his required curriculum by taking a sheet of paper, marking it into sections by curriculum areas (e.g., math, literacy) and then writing *from memory* the goals or standards for the children in his classroom. If the teacher does not know this information without looking it up in a curriculum guide or manual, he is unlikely to recognize opportunities inherent in the project topic for children to accomplish these goals. He is also less likely to integrate these while teaching on the fly in the heat of project work. For example, if the teacher does not know that gathering and representing data is a curriculum goal, when a child says that more kids have Velcro fasteners than ties, he is

unlikely to respond with, "I know a way we could write that down so we can see. Would you like me to show you?"

If a teacher does not have a clear understanding of the content, skills, and dispositions that are supposed to be taught, a first step toward deepening project work would be to solve this problem and create a list. Although this sounds basic and one would hope that this has already been provided to teachers, my training experiences have revealed that many teachers do not have a clear understanding of exactly what children need to learn and what they are to teach. The first step in anticipating opportunities for integration, then, is to obtain this information. Even if teachers are in a program where curriculum goals are not required or expected, they should have goals in mind for children in their classrooms. There may be learning standards, such as the Common Core State Standards, a teacher's manual for a required math or literacy program, and sometimes another list from the report card. Often standards are general, but children's progress is assessed using a checklist that is more specific. For example, there may be a general kindergarten standard such as "Use concepts that include number recognition, counting, and one-to-one correspondence." In addition, children may be evaluated on a report card that includes items such as "Recognizes and writes numerals 1–30" and "Can make sets." Sometimes a content program (such as a math book or reading book) may contain additional knowledge and skills that are not required to be taught in every local program because textbook publishers include everything they feel that any school might want so that their books are applicable to a large number of schools. Sometimes topics in a required curriculum program are introduced to build awareness; mastery is not expected. Just because there is a page on reading pie charts in the manual, this might not mean that a teacher is responsible for teaching it or that all children must master that concept at this time.

A teacher in a program that has manuals for required curriculum materials, a separate list of standards, and an assessment system with another list of goals (which may or may not be coordinated) will find it less frustrating and more effective to work with a consolidated comprehensive list. The teacher can make one consolidated list of all requirements and their sources and then seek assistance from supervisors to clarify discrepancies. A clear understanding of what is to be taught is essential. Training on integration of standards may be available for teachers, or they may find published tables that correlate required curriculum programs with local or state standards. Such resources will help with this consolidation task. The list resulting from this task will be extremely helpful in deepening project work, but it will also simplify and improve planning for units, thematic studies, and even spontaneous learning opportunities. It is a good step toward increasing intentionality of teaching.

Sometimes an examination of required curriculum will result in the discovery that there is a particular sequence for the introduction of concepts. In multiage early childhood classrooms, this is not usually an issue. Kindergarten and primary curriculum guides, however, are often arranged chronologically. The teacher will need to determine if knowledge or a skill has to be introduced in a particular sequence. Often the order is flexible so teachers may introduce skills when they are most meaningful to children instead of following the order in the manual. For example, in the Shoe Project, measuring feet to determine the correct shoe size is relevant to the children. If learning how to use standard units of measurement (such as inches) or even nonstandard units (such as building cubes or straws) is a curriculum goal, then this is a perfect opportunity to teach the skill. Anticipating what skill might be needed, then teaching it at the time children must use it maximizes the children's engagement. Even when the skill requires explicit teaching, a teacher can teach it during more formal times of the day, then use project work as the "practice time" for integration and application of the newly developed or previously taught skill.

Generally, a teacher who has required sequenced curriculum content can integrate it into project work in one of five ways:

1. *Rearrange sequence of instruction.* Teach a required skill at the time of interest in project work instead of waiting to introduce the skill when it appears in a timed curriculum sequence. This brings engagement to the topic. The same curriculum materials may be used in a more formal part of the day but within the same days or week that the skill will be needed in project work.

2. *Teach the skill during formal instructional times using authentic project content.* For example, during a small-group time that is designated for math, a kindergarten teacher might show children how to make a data chart of their types of shoes as the math activity instead of the prepared curriculum activity. This may also require rearranging sequence.

3. *Teach the skill on the fly during project work.* Take advantage of opportunities to introduce and use skills as children are investigating or representing. This may occur during more informal project time.

4. *Teach the skill at formal instructional times and then use the project work for application and practice.* Use the project experiences to provide opportunities for meaningful use of knowledge and skills. (This works especially well if a required topic has already been introduced to the students before the project occurs.)

5. *Document achievement of required curriculum goals and standards in project work.* Use the documentation to show effectiveness of integrating goals and standards into project work.

All of these strategies enhance curriculum because children are learning knowledge and skills at a point when they want to know the information and can readily see why it would be useful to know. In other words, it is the tying together of the academic goal or standard to content of interest to the child that engages the child in learning the academic skill. Figure 4.1 illustrates a way to think about this process of tying together content of interest and curriculum goals. The child's engagement in the topic enables the goals and standards to become relevant to the child.

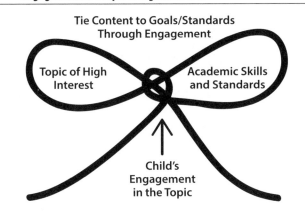

Understanding of Children

To intentionally plan for project work that fosters children's deep engagement, teachers also need clear understanding of the interests and daily experiences of their children, as discussed in Chapter 3. Just knowing curriculum goals and standards is not enough. As teachers create the comprehensive list of what they are supposed to teach, they can note what knowledge and skills coincide with the interests and lives of the children in their classroom. In other words, teachers can think carefully about what aspects of the curriculum are most likely to engage their children. In the Shoe Project example, the teacher's awareness of her children's interest in their shoes guided her choice of activities to build background knowledge (Phase I of the project approach). Her own knowledge of the extensive variation in shoes led her to think that this aspect of a study of shoes might be an effective way for children to sort objects by attributes and encourage children to have a focused discussion with other children.

CREATING AND USING AN ANTICIPATORY PLANNING WEB

Once a teacher has a clear understanding of required curriculum content and standards and of the interests and daily experiences of the children, she can apply these to a topic by creating an anticipatory planning web. This teacher web (completed by the teacher, not by the children) provides a way to prepare for (or anticipate) opportunities to integrate required curriculum in response to children's interests. It also enables the teacher to anticipate which experts or field trips might be beneficial and what materials or supplies would be handy to have on hand.

Webbing is a common technique for planning for emergent curriculum (Jones & Nimmo, 1994). It requires creative brainstorming and provides a loose map (not detailed directions) of the concepts within the topic. Which concepts are investigated within that map, or where the project might go, will be determined by student interest and the questions the children ask during their investigation. This web can be consulted throughout the project process and will lessen the chance that teachers will miss opportunities for integrating skill building and practice.

Creating an anticipatory web also enables a teacher to think deeply about what she knows about the topic and to identify content that she doesn't know. Although being a colearner is an important part of the role of the teacher (Dewey, 1897), the more the teacher knows about the content, the better she is able to anticipate the appropriate learning experiences and avoid passing on misinformation. According to the Math and Science Partnership, Knowledge Management and Dissemination website (Horizon Research Inc., 2010), a teacher's knowledge of content has a number of direct and indirect effects on classroom practice. A teacher's confidence in a topic affects interactions with children within the project. In research of classrooms at a variety of grade levels, teachers with deeper content knowledge were more likely than those with weaker knowledge to pose questions, suggest alternative explanations, and propose additional inquiries for students.

Webbing or concept mapping has also been associated with more effective teaching outcomes. It is especially appropriate for emergent curriculum. Other forms of planning tend to be more linear. Linear planning begins with a list of goals, activities, methods or strategies, and materials. Then the activities are introduced within the classroom. This locks the teacher into the planned activities regardless of children's interest or curiosity. This is not a practical way to plan for project work. When using an anticipatory planning web, the teacher begins with the concepts inherent in a topic, then identifies all the possible ways the project might go.

In observing deep project work I am often impressed with the skill of experienced project teachers to integrate academic concepts in response to children's engagement. Although this teaching on the fly looks like a spontaneous response to the child's needs, it has usually been preceded by the teacher's firm grasp of curriculum goals and an analysis of the topic. In this way the teacher has become mentally prepared and is watching for opportunities to integrate curriculum. For example, during a conversation about differences in shoes, a child might talk about the size of his daddy's shoes. Because the teacher has anticipated an opportunity to integrate numeral recognition and the relationship to differences in shoe sizes, she can respond to the child immediately by talking with him about sizes. She might ask the child how he can look for the size in his own shoe, in the teacher's shoe, and in his daddy's shoes. By this immediate response, the teacher connects what interests the child to the academic goal. Or if the curriculum goal that the teacher has in mind is "Collect information to answer questions" or "Compare data in picture graphs, identifying more, fewer, same" (Virginia Department of Education, 2007), she could respond at that moment of peak interest with a suggestion that the children might create a picture graph to compare shoe sizes. In each of these cases the concept is an authentic application of the academic goal to the world of shoes, and the child's engagement and interest in the topic enables him to see the relevance of learning the academic goal. When beginning the planning process by imagining on a bow tying topic concepts to academic skills and standards (see Figure 4.1), teachers find it easier to create and support authentic activities.

Teachers who want to deepen project work will find that a more detailed anticipatory planning web will make it easier for them to extend children's interests and integrate curriculum goals and standards such as the CCSS. A step-by-step guide to help you create an anticipatory planning web is provided in the sections that follow.

Step 1: Map Concepts

In this step you will anticipate concepts that might be encountered in the project topic. To begin, write the main study topic in the center of a blank page using a marker. Draw a circle around it. In the same color add concepts about the topic in a web format and connect these to the circle with a straight line. For example, for the topic "shoes," concepts might include "Shoes have parts," "Shoes come in different sizes," "Shoes are bought" (see Figure 4.2). Keep your focus on concepts about shoes; do not list activities for children to do with the shoes. You will do this later in the process. Most experienced teachers will naturally think of learning experiences that have been successful in the past. Although it is difficult not to think of those lessons, it is more helpful if you can concentrate on identifying concepts in the topic first and reserve planning activities until you can see what children are most interested in.

If it is difficult to list concepts, teachers have found it helpful to identify concepts by imagining a book for elementary-age children entitled, for example, *All About Shoes* (or whatever topic is being considered for project work) and thinking of the concepts one might find in that book. The book would not include activities to do with shoes, only content about the world of shoes.

As this concept map evolves, you will find out that you know a lot, a little, or just a few things about the topic being considered. If you discover that your own knowledge about the topic is limited, you may want to stop the planning process until you have time to read up on the topic. For example, children may have discovered a cicada shell on the playground and become quite excited about it. The topic has great promise for a project because the children are highly engaged and you know that "learning what living things need" is a science standard. However, as you make a web of the cicada, you discover that you know very little. Is it an insect? Is that a shell, or is that the dead body? Has something eaten the insides out of this shell? Are cicadas dangerous? A little research on the Internet can fill in the blanks in your knowledge base, and the anticipatory planning web will

Figure 4.2. Step 1: Map the concepts related to the project.

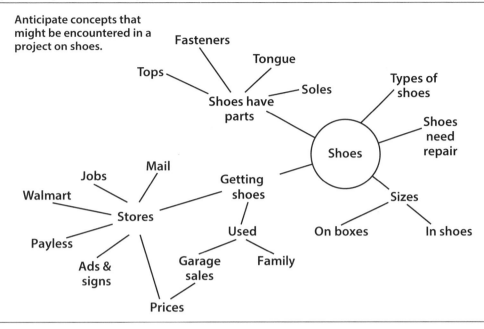

An anticipatory planning web with topic concepts and curriculum goals side by side will remind you of where opportunities might occur for children to learn a specific knowledge or skill in the project. Learning opportunities might include reading the shoe sizes printed in the shoes and on the boxes or the prices of shoes shown in store ads or signs in shoe stores. It is important during this stage of the planning that you focus on identifying opportunities for children to meaningfully encounter knowledge and skills, not to start thinking of teacher-directed activities. By looking on the concept web for those concepts that authentically connect to specific knowledge and/or skills (or an abbreviated version of the appropriate standard) and writing them next to the concept on the web in a new color, you will be able to generate appropriate, authentic learning experiences for the children in the next step of the process. For example, next to "Sizes" you would write "Numeral recognition" (see Figure 4.3)

While doing this step in making the web, you should keep your focus on identifying concepts in which the children might see the usefulness of relevant knowledge and skills. At the same time, you will be able to identify opportunities for children to naturally practice the application of that knowledge and skills. The goal of this step is to

be richer and more helpful as you now have an idea of what opportunities for learning knowledge, skills, and dispositions might occur in this project.

Step 2: Identify Opportunities to Integrate Standards and Goals

In this step you will find authentic opportunities to integrate standards and goals into the project. With your comprehensive list of the knowledge and skills that are included in your standards and required curriculum goals, you can now think about which of these goals connect naturally and authentically with the concepts inherent in the topic and write these onto the web in a new color. For example, the world of shoes is a topic in which children would encounter the need for "numeral recognition" ("Differentiate numerals from letters and recognize some single digit written numerals," from Illinois Early Learning and Development Standards, Preschool Benchmark 6A.ECe [Illinois State Board of Education, 2013]). Numerals are needed for shoe sizes, prices, sales signs, and inventories. As children encounter the concepts of shoe sizes, places where one gets shoes, and selling and buying shoes, the need to use numerals will become clear to the children and motivate them to learn and practice using numerals.

Figure 4.3. Step 2: Identify where goals and standards naturally occur.

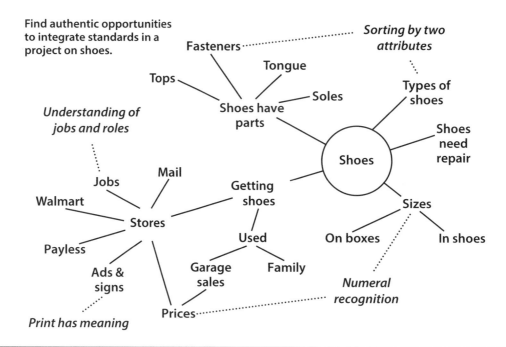

find authentic intersections between the concepts and the curriculum. This will enable children to see the curriculum goals as meaningful and worth learning.

Step 3: Tie Together Topic Concepts and Goals or Standards

In this step you will think about how goals and standards can be tied to the topic concepts of the project. Teachers have found it helpful to review the web they have created with the concepts and the curriculum goals in Steps 1 and 2 and draw bows where goals and concepts come together. Figure 4.4 shows how an anticipatory planning web looks when this thinking process to identify ways to integrate curriculum goals (and standards) is repeated to create a detailed anticipatory planning web. You can examine your web and, using a marker, literally tie concepts to knowledge and skills. The anticipatory planning web at this point has a bow at each place on the web where concepts and knowledge and skills come together, indicating that these are opportunities to capitalize on child engagement.

Step 4: Identify Possible Project Activities

In this step you will make a list of possible authentic project activities to extend interest and tie goals/standards to content of interest. You can now focus on planning those engaging learning experiences that will move the project forward. Your web now has *concepts* in one color and *knowledge and skills* in another, with bows identifying where a concept and a standard/goal come together, such as "Sizes" and "Numeral recognition." You can now think of possible authentic learning experiences for children that integrate these and might also function as a good activity for building background knowledge. Some of these experiences can be used in Phase I of the project approach to build background knowledge and determine direction of the project. You can use some as opportunity arises during the investigation in response to children's interests and questions, and some as teacher-initiated activities in other parts of the day such as at circle time or reading time. It is important that you strive to keep the activities realistic and authentic. For example, you could plan to show children where sizes are located on shoes, and then

Figure 4.4. Step 3: Tie together concepts and goals or standards.

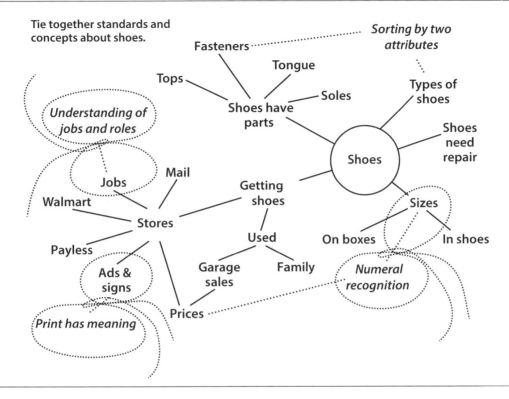

sort the shoes by sizes as they would be in a store. Although this is teacher directed, it is an authentic, or real, task performed in shoe stores. This activity shows children the usefulness of numerals and motivates them to learn. They are likely to repeat the activity at home, gaining additional practice with numerals. The task is likely to be highly engaging for children.

Contrast this with a common shoe-theme activity that is not authentic. In this activity a teacher prepares construction paper cutouts of pairs of shoes. On one shoe in each pair she places dots. On the other shoe in the pair she writes a numeral. She asks the children to make pairs of the paper shoes by matching the numerals and dots. Although this activity is not harmful, it fails to engage the children in the same way, does not demonstrate the value of learning numerals or using them in the real world, and requires teacher monitoring for some children to complete the task. This activity and similar file-folder types of activities frequently emerge in training discussions as good activities, and teachers will often jump to these types of

activities as they think about a project on a topic of shoes. By delaying the brainstorming of activities and experiences to this stage in the planning process, you are more likely to generate authentic and meaningful ideas. Anticipating these opportunities for integration will enable you to be prepared with introductory lessons, materials, and supplies and also to interact supportively with children as they do their project work.

Figure 4.5 illustrates a way that you can again use the bow, this time to help you generate authentic learning activities. Selecting a pair of concepts and goals that you have tied together with a bow, you can think about an activity or activities that would engage children. On the right tail of the tie you can list changes that you might make. One way to do this is to think about what changes you might make in the environment, or what provocations might be helpful, or what specific questions you might ask. On the left tail of the tie, you can list expectations for what the children will do. Figure 4.5 shows what this might look like. For example, you might plan to devote circle time to children examining and talking about their shoes (Environment: *Time to look at shoe*). While children are looking at and talking about their shoes, you might ask questions (Questions: *Are the shoes of all our boys and girls the same size? When you pick out a shoe, how do you know how big it is?*). You might also challenge the children (Provocation: *How could we find out how many children wear size 6 shoes?*).

In Appendix E a worksheet is provided for you to practice tying together concepts and goals. Although it is unlikely that you will use such detail as adding bows in each web you make, thinking about the parts of the tie is helpful in shaping planning and being prepared to respond to children's engagement. Most teachers simply review the bows on the web and make a separate list of possible activities (see bottom of Figure 4.5). As a project progresses, teachers have found it helpful to revisit this planning web as the focus of the project shifts and opportunities emerge. Revisiting the web helps you think about what you might do to deepen children's experiences and extend their thinking.

Step 5: Follow the Children's Lead

In this last step of planning you will alter the web according to the children's interest. After the initial experiences occur, children's interest will begin to emerge. You can identify which concepts are of the most interest to the most children by observing their involvement in these initial learning experiences. If children appear to be more interested in shoe repair than shoe stores or where shoes come from, then shoe repair can become the topic of the project, maximizing the children's initiation, engagement, and decision making. Many teachers find it helpful to physically cut out the section of the planning web that has become the focus of the project and move it to the center of the web. For example, shoe repair is moved to the center of the web to remind you and any additional staff or parents of the new topic (see Figure 4.6). Instead of the Shoe Project, the children are now involved in a deep investigation of the Shoe Repair Project. This last step in the planning process, the narrowing of the topic to match children's interest, is when the

Figure 4.5. Step 4: Identify initial project activities to build background knowledge.

Make a list of authentic activities to extend interest and tie goals/standards to content of interest.

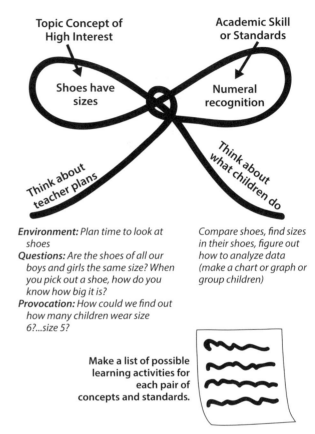

topic becomes a project. Narrowing the topic to match the children's engagement, then encouraging children to develop and find answers to their questions, and following children's lead increases child decision making and engagement. It moves the learning experience to the right on the continuum to project work (see Chapter 2).

When you cut out and move the area of interest to the center of the anticipatory planning web, many of the concepts and useful and meaningful applications of knowledge and skills will remain applicable to this new, narrower topic. However, other concepts or applications will be replaced, dropped, or moved to another, newly added concept. It is more important to empower children to make decisions and direct their investigation than for you, as the teacher, to do all the activities that you anticipated doing, although sometimes this can be difficult for a teacher to accept. In one project

Figure 4.6. Step 5: Follow the children's lead in narrowing the project topic.

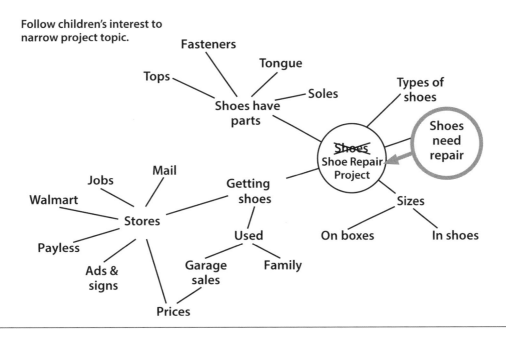

in a 2nd-grade classroom, the teacher had anticipated a project on fish would focus on aquariums. Instead, the students were more interested in the body of the fish and the project on fish turned into a project on bones and skeletons. By adding new concepts related to this new interest and shifting activities to integrate different learning goals, the teacher was able to still cover a significant amount of required curriculum and the students had a great project, even without aquariums.

Remember to revisit your anticipatory planning web throughout the project and adjust and add as the project emerges. A summary sheet of how to go through the process of creating an anticipatory planning web is included in Appendix F.

USING LESSON PLANS WITH PROJECTS

A common question regarding planning and project work is how to incorporate the project work into lesson plans. There are three lesson plan formats included in *Windows on Learning: Documenting Young Children's Work* (Helm, Beneke, & Steinheimer, 2007, pp. 154–157). The first sample lesson plan is based on a time schedule, and the other two are based on weekly planning using domains. Each lesson plan has a column or section for listing curriculum and assessment goals that are the focus of the week. These can be stated as domains of learning, Common Core State Standards, or required curriculum goals from mandatory curriculum programs, and can be part of advanced lesson planning. A second column is provided in the weekly forms for flexibility in planning. This space evolves as the week progresses and can be used for project work, including teaching strategies for specific students' learning goals (target zones) and planned activities related to project work, and opportunities for extended work experiences related to the project that will run over several days or plans for extension of child-initiated learning experiences (emergent learning experiences). These forms are designed to accompany the anticipatory planning web described in this chapter, which shows how standards and documentation connect with concepts of the project or unit being studied. The second column is filled in as the week goes by, enabling the teacher to be responsive to student direction of the project. Using this space, the teacher can reflect on observations and documentation from each day to plan materials and experiences to be ready for the next day.

A third column helps the teacher think about the environment and what is available in the classroom on a daily basis. A fourth column is provided for planning for large-group times, building community, communicating with each other, sharing progress, and so on. The information in these last two columns will evolve as the project progresses.

It is not necessary to use these planning forms or any specific form for projects. These may not fit with your program; however, some type of organized preplanning is necessary so teachers have a clear sense of how the learning goals can occur in the classroom. The best lesson-planning format provides opportunities for planning ahead and preparation of resources and materials, while keeping portions of the planning flexible and open to be responsive to the direction of the project.

As the learning experience of a project progresses, you can determine whether to introduce knowledge and skills before children need them in their project work or to introduce them during a project experience, or whether the project will provide mainly practice of skills previously introduced during the year (with no new skill introduction). For some children and some projects each of these strategies might be used: you might introduce the knowledge or skill before the child will use it, demonstrate and provide coaching at the time it will be used, and then allow the child plenty of time for practice. In any case, even when the project goes in a surprising direction, students will always benefit from the planning and careful thought about integration of academic goals in project work. In my experience, deep project work just does not happen without teachers thinking deeply.

CHAPTER 5

Questions, Questions, Questions

Questions are a key component of deep project work, and they appear throughout the project phases. During Phase I children's questions reveal the depth of interest in a topic and assist the teacher in determining the viability of a topic for project work. Questions determine the direction of a project or what particular aspect of a topic will be most productive for deep project work. For example, if the children are exploring the topic of farms and the children keep asking questions about the combine-harvester and the tractor, the teacher can see that the children are most interested in and curious about farm machinery. Farm machinery becomes the focus of the project. As the project progresses, individual questions can reveal children's individual interests in the different aspects of a topic. For example, one child may be very interested in the computer in the combine-harvester cab.

When the children have a good list or web of their questions, Phase I is ended, and the stage is set for investigating in Phase II (refer to Figure 3.1). Children's questions are reviewed and analyzed by the teacher as field site visits are planned and experts chosen. Using questions to shape these learning experiences assures that they will make sense and have meaning for the children. Children use questions as their primary way to connect with experts, both those whom they see on the field site visit and also those who visit their classroom. When children have questions to ask, the experience moves from a passive learning experience to an active child-driven experience. These questions often result in additional spontaneous questions. Revisiting questions often results in more follow-up questions, which then open additional avenues for investigation. In Phase III teachers use questions and answers captured at the beginning and end of a project to assess what

children have learned and the effectiveness of the project. The focus on children's questions is one of the central characteristics of project work that distinguishes it from teacher-directed units and themes.

QUESTIONS AND MBE SCIENCE

Asking and finding answers to children's questions can be enormously powerful for building mind and brain capacity in children. Focusing on children's questions enables a teacher to be sure that the project experience meets most of the instructional guidelines of Mind, Brain, and Education Science. Guideline 6, which is more relevant for topic selection, is not addressed here.

Instructional Guidelines

1. Learning Environments. Children's questions and questions that teachers ask children can provide a structure for intellectual conversations. The process of collecting questions provides a purpose for interesting and authentic conversations between children and their teacher and among children. Project questions provide "something to talk about." Predicting answers to questions and sharing personal theories can create lively debate. Generating authentic questions provides a clear vision of what children want to know and makes conversations student-centered and dynamic.

2. Sense and Meaning. Finding the answers to questions they ask is an authentic experience for young children. Because the questions come from children based on what they already know and want to know, the questions are more likely to have meaning for the children. Children's questions also provide a natural context for the teacher to assess prior knowledge and to determine the culturally based neural network (knowledge) that children already have about the topic. For example, if a child asks a question about how the shoe salesperson knows what size shoes are needed, the teacher now knows that the child has some experience with shopping for shoes and also some idea of the role of sizes in fitting a shoe. This knowledge helps the teacher connect project experiences with what the child already knows, increasing relevance of the topic.

3. Memory. Children's questions utilize the three systems of long-term memory: associative memory, value-laden memory, and survival-value memory. When children ask questions and then find their own answers, they must think about what they know about a topic, their *associations* with the topic (*associative memory)*. If they have no prior knowledge, they are unlikely to ask a question. If a teacher structures the gathering of questions so that they are authentic and not just a list produced without much thought, then those questions will come from the children's curiosity and interest. They are more likely to be *emotionally important (value laden)* to the children, also enhancing long-term memory. This is especially helpful if the teacher discourages asking the same type of question over and over again (e.g., How many doors does the fire truck have? How many hoses does the fire truck have? How many tires does the fire truck have?). If the questions and their answers are important to children, then they will be motivated to record the questions by writing or drawing and to answer them by collecting and analyzing data. In this way children will see those academic skills *as survival skills*, ways that they can accomplish what they want to accomplish. Storing and retrieving information become habits of mind.

4. Attention Spans. Asking questions and finding answers to those questions are inherently engaging. Collecting, recording, and sharing the answers provide opportunities for children to reflect on what they have learned. Because the questions are the

children's, they are more attentive and will persist for a longer time in tasks involved in finding answers.

5. The Social Nature of Learning. Because questions are collected by the group and answers are shared with the group, the children are required to communicate and to participate in the group process. Children share their perceptions and information with the whole group so everyone can learn together.

7. Orchestrated Immersion. Questions enable the teacher to make sure that projects are orchestrated immersion learning experiences. The teacher can use the children's questions as the basis for decisions about which experiences and which experts to include in the project. In this way the teacher individualizes the project to accommodate the differences in brain processes and preferences. Because questions come from individuals, each child can approach and connect with the topic at her own level of understanding. New information is received and processed according to the preferences of each child. For example, one child might ask a question about where the stamps are stored in the post office and then make a drawing of the stamp drawer to record the answer. Another child in the same class may have a question about how the zip code tells the postal carrier how to make sure the letter goes to his grandma's house. This child may be interested in a map of zip code zones and may create a list of zip codes using the map. As the children share what they have learned with the class, the teacher can be like an orchestra conductor, integrating the strengths and skills of each learner to maximize the project as a learning experience for all of the children.

8. Active Processes. Finding the answers to questions generated by the children engages learners and makes projects active rather than passive learning experiences. Instead of just listening to an expert give a talk, the children ask questions and actively listen for answers. When children have specific questions about a topic, they try to find the answers to those questions. They examine artifacts closely, observe processes, and design experiments. They use higher-order thinking skills as they plan how to find answers. They often design experiments and create surveys. Then when they learn the answers, they decide how to record and communicate what they have learned. In the case of very young children, they apply what they have learned to their creative play scenarios. By encouraging the children to develop and answer their own questions, a teacher helps children develop investigation and representation skills that they will be able to use in other learning experiences.

9. Metacognition. When a child is asked if she has a question, she has to think about what she does not know. That is beginning metacognition, or "thinking about her own thinking." When a teacher takes the time to talk with children about what they have learned (making lists or webs) and what they have found out (providing ways to showcase how they recorded or represented answers to their questions), he is drawing attention to their ability to direct and focus their thinking. Revisiting a list of questions gives children time to reflect on their grasp of new concepts. In the same way, a teacher can ask questions of children about their work. For example, a teacher can ask a group of children to explain why they decided to use certain materials for a structure.

10. Learning Throughout the Life Span. This instructional guideline emphasizes the continuous nature of learning from year to year, rather than age- or grade-level segmentations of learning. Each child is on an individual journey of development and skill acquisition that begins at birth and continues throughout adulthood. Although age can predict where a child might be, the prediction is not always applicable to every child. For example, one would not expect a 4-year-old to be able to read a zip code, decipher a zip code zone map, and explain how the zip code directs a letter to grandma in Florida. One would be unlikely to see these skills on a list of milestones or benchmarks for 4-year-olds. In project work, individual children come into the project wherever they are in their own journey. Because of that, the typical age predictions of skills and

development are often less relevant for children doing project work. Developmentally appropriate practice (DAP) as defined by the National Association for the Education of Young Children (Copple & Bredekamp, 2009) provides guidance regarding age appropriateness of learning experiences; however, DAP also advocates meeting children where they are, as individuals and as a group, and then supporting each child in attaining challenging and achievable goals. A teacher needs to consider what is individually appropriate and what is culturally appropriate for each child, including language and literacy skills, understanding of the topic, and cognitive functioning. When children ask and answer their own questions, and answer thought-provoking questions by their teacher, they provide information to the teacher about where they are on that continuous progression of learning.

Growth of Questioning Skills

Questioning is referred to by Chouirnard (2007) as a type of Information Requesting Mechanism (IRM). These mechanisms include not only verbal questions but also gestures, expressions, and vocalizations. IRMs enable children to access information and play an important role in cognitive development. Children use IRMs as young as 12 months. When children request information, they are attempting to fill a gap in what they know, resolve an inconsistency in what they think, or solve a problem.

The importance of questions to children's development can be seen in how frequently children initiate the behavior. According to Chouirnard's research (2007), question asking is absolutely central to children's daily interactions with other people. Young children (ages 1–5) ask between 76 and 95 questions per hour when in conversation with adults. Asking questions enables children to access information at the very point that they need that information. This empowers the adult to provide the answer or to help children find it. This "targeting" of information and assistance to the exact time that children need them enables the adult to make a significant contribution to the intellectual growth of children. According to

Vygotsky, when an adult (or in some cases a peer) can identify exactly what children need—that zone of proximal development described in Chapter 2—then the adult can give a child an experience that encourages and advances the child's learning (L. E. Berk & Winsler, 1995). Young children are good at helping adults define that zone because they ask a great many information-seeking questions and they get informative answers as a result. If children don't get an informative response, they keep asking. The content of children's questions parallels their conceptual advances, and the content shifts with an exchange and over the course of development to reflect what they are learning. Questions shape the way adults talk to and interact with children. Adults will volunteer additional information in about a quarter of their responses to children's questions. The adult perhaps identifies that the child is not quite able to frame a question for the exact information needed (Chouinard, 2007). According to Dutch researcher Lotte Henrichs, when adults in children's lives recognize 3-6-year-olds as full-fledged conversation partners and take their questions seriously, they establish an early basis for the development of academic language, which will contribute to school success (NWO, 2010).

The growth in children's ability to ask questions is continuous, and it may be helpful for teachers to know typical development of this skill The types of questions that children ask increase in diversity during the early years:

- "What that" or "dat" questions at 21–24 months
- "Where" questions at 26–32 months
- "Is" and "do" questions at 37–42 months
- "When," "why," and "how" questions most likely at 42–49 months (Linder, 2008)

So in project work a teacher might see the majority of toddler's IFMs to be gestures, nonverbal indicators, and vocalizations, with some children asking "what's that" kind of questions. In preschool the questions might begin with labeling but progress all the way to "where," "when," "how," and "why" questions.

ELICITING CHILDREN'S PROJECT QUESTIONS

One of the biggest challenges in doing projects with young children is identifying the most meaningful areas of investigation for a group of children. Questions, or IRMs, are the key to deep project work. However, getting questions from children who are just learning how to ask questions is not easy. In observing teachers who have had deep project experiences, I found that they use a few strategies that are especially effective.

Build a Common Background Knowledge

In Chapter 3 some general guidelines were provided for facilitating meaningful conversations with children about a topic, including setting expectations, modeling, and considering room arrangement and group sizes. All of these strategies support intellectual conversations, which can enhance the probability that productive questions will emerge. Ways to focus children on a topic were also discussed. Once a topic is identified, it is still helpful to work on developing general background knowledge of the children, as mentioned in Chapter 4. It is important to make sure that everyone in the classroom has some understanding of the topic. This is sometimes referred to as "messing around with the topic." This builds children's vocabulary and creates a knowledge base for some children who may not have had experience with the topic. During this part of Phase I of the project approach, the project has some similarities to thematic teaching. The process is more teacher-directed at this point. Learning experiences that can be used to build background knowledge include telling personal stories and reading books related to the topic. Books may be fictional if realistic, but informational books work best. Books for adults or older children that contain photos and diagrams to look at can be included. A field trip, as opposed to a focused field site visit, which occurs later in the project, can also be helpful. A walkthrough or a general tour will help children become acquainted with a topic. Videos and photographs can be viewed, and a few artifacts collected. First-time drawings can be done. (See also Helm & Katz, 2011, pp. 23–25.) There is a fine line between providing enough teacher-directed experiences to build background knowledge and taking over the direction of the project. However, to enable deep project work, children, especially very young children, are unlikely to ask productive questions if they have little or no vocabulary and background knowledge. It is not unusual in a deep project with preschoolers to have Phase I last 2 weeks before children are able to ask productive, higher-level questions. A strategy for deepening project work, then, is to spend a little more time during this phase. When the teacher sees the children begin to use vocabulary related to the topic and spontaneous conversations about the topic occur, then that is a good time to formally focus on getting questions recorded for investigation.

Teach How to Ask Questions

If a teacher has established conversation routines and is able to have a good intellectual conversation with children about a topic, the questions will often just flow. This is especially true for kindergarteners and primary-age children. At this point the teacher can introduce the idea of recording the questions as a list or create a web. With preschoolers, doing this in small groups or talking to children one at a time is more productive. This encourages all children to participate instead of just a few. Webs and lists can then be combined and shared during a whole-group meeting.

To get questions from younger children, the teacher can observe children's interest and comments they make and reframe some of the children's thoughts into questions. She can ask, "Is that something you would like to know about?" "Would you like to know how to use that?" She can then state that as a question. With novice question-makers, this can be done individually, and then brought to the group later as "Anna's question," which is then added to the list or web.

Teachers should not hesitate to ask their own questions. Modeling curiosity is one of the best ways to foster children's disposition to be curious. The teacher can also be more direct and model wondering by focusing the children on her own thinking process. For example, the teacher could say,

- I am wondering about . . . (e.g., what makes the tractor run). What do you think?
- I wonder who . . . (e.g., brings the lunches to the cafeteria).
- I wonder how . . . (e.g., the farmer gets the corn into the silo).
- I wonder where . . . (e.g., the veterinarian keeps the medicine).
- I wonder when . . . (e.g., the milk comes to the store).

After demonstrating some of these, the teacher can also use these question stems to serve as prompts for young children by starting the question, then stopping on a high note so that children will know they can finish the sentence for the teacher, for example, "I wonder who . . . ."

The teacher should not hesitate to directly provoke questions by asking the children: "What do you suppose this is for?" "How do you think this fits with that?" The teacher can show a photo or model and ask, "What would you like to know about [situation, item]?" Another helpful question in preparation for a field site visit or expert visitor is, "What would you like _____ to tell us?"

Learn from This Example of Project Questions

Here are some questions from the Spider Project in Amber Forrest's class of 4-year-olds at Seeds of Faith Preschool in Clive, Iowa. They are typical of questions that occur in project work. The spider project began when Amber noticed that many children were excited about the daddy longlegs they discovered in the playhouse on the playground. Some children were screaming and running from the daddy longlegs, and some were grabbing it and observing it. This prompted them to investigate daddy longlegs. Amber did an Internet search for daddy longlegs and discovered that they weren't really spiders. When she shared this with the children and showed what she had found, the children asked, "What makes a spider?" The following are more 4-year-olds' questions from the Spider Project:

- How do spiders make egg sacks? —Jaime, Luke L., Peyton, Andrew, Mia
- Why are spiders big? —Ben, Abby
- How do spiders eat? —Josie, Cael
- How do water spiders swim? —Sam H.
- What do spiders do when there are loud noises, like fireworks? —Kevin
- How do spiders swim on hot water? —Anna
- Why do they have two body parts? —Tommy
- Why do spiders have eight legs? —Graham
- Why do they have big and little legs? —Brolen
- Why do they have little eyes? —Mollie
- Why do they have pinchers in front of their mouths? —Laney
- Do spiders have ears? How do they hear? —DeDe
- Do they eat their babies? —Addy
- Where do spiders go in the fall? —Theo
- Why do they hide in the grass? —Lucy
- Why are spiders scared of people? —Gehrig
- Why do they have spider webs? —Chance
- Why do they build new homes? —Shaina
- Do they eat their spider webs? —Gabe

These questions reveal that the children have already gained quite a lot of knowledge about spiders because Amber took the time to build background knowledge (see Figure 5.1). She also continued to collect and record questions throughout the project and not just at the beginning. The result is that the questions go beyond "what is" to "why" and "how." As children discussed and predicted answers, they also used higher-level thinking skills such as wondering where spiders go in the fall when it gets cold or why spiders might be afraid of people and hide. The Spider Project is also discussed in Chapter 6, where the children's representations reveal how much they learned as they found answers to their questions.

Categorize Questions

A teacher's first review of children's questions usually focuses on what aspect of the content is most interesting to children and which area is the most interesting to which children. For that reason, Amber recorded the names of children with

Figure 5.1. Providing many opportunities for children to explore a topic builds background knowledge and the vocabulary needed to ask productive questions.

their questions. Determining areas of special interest is helpful for gathering resources and for identifying experts to come to the classroom and field sites that the class might visit. Some teachers use the grouping of questions according to subtopics as a way to group children of similar interests for field site visits. Projects in preschool usually flow better and keep momentum going if children are able to move in and out of project work and are also able to vary what aspect of the optional project work they want to participate in on a daily basis. The teacher will summarize the availability of project work for the day and ask who might like to do it. This enables children to float in and out of different learning experiences related to the topic. That is what happened in the Seed Store Project in Michelle's preschool classroom. Children kindergarten age and older are able to sustain interest in a subtopic and persist through more complex investigations and representations that extend over days. These children often enjoy forming committees or teams that focus on a specific aspect of the project. These groups can take responsibility for finding answers and reporting to the whole class.

Although all of the children's project questions are important and should be recognized and recorded, some questions are more helpful for guiding project work than others. As children are learning how to ask questions and find answers, questions commonly emerge that are not really questions or cannot be answered. When planning how to facilitate investigation in Phase II, taking time to more thoroughly analyze and categorize questions is a good place to start. Sheilah Jelly (2001) developed categories for children's questions, which have been helpful to many project teachers. Following are some of Jelly's categories adapted to guiding projects with young children:

- *Fact questions* can't be answered through children's independent investigation. These are simply requests for information that the teacher or another person might have and the child does not (e.g., Where did you find that daddy longlegs? or How many horses do you have on your farm?). Productive responses to such questions include answering the question factually or helping the child ask someone who knows the answer. If the teacher doesn't know the answer, then he can respond with, "Who do you think we could talk to in order to get that information?" For young children, learning the names of things is enormously powerful. Once they know the name of something, they can talk about it, draw conclusions about the named item, or ask others to define characteristics. Naming supports intellectual thought.

- *Comment questions* are not real questions even though they are worded like questions (e.g., "Why are spiders so smart that they can make webs?"). These are more than likely statements of observation. The child might really be saying, "I see that spiders make webs and that looks hard to do." Sometimes they are statements of awe. The child might really be thinking, "Wow, spiders can make webs with their bodies. That is awesome!" For comment questions teachers can acknowledge them and respond as if they were comments (e.g., "I think it is really cool that spiders can make webs too."). If the question was really a comment, the child will appreciate that his attempt to communicate was successful. If the

child is not satisfied with this response, he will often come back with a real question.

- *Inquiry questions* are questions whose answers can be discovered by young children in the ways that they learn best. These include opportunities for children to independently investigate by touching, feeling, listening, smelling, or looking closely. These are very promising for deep project work, and a teacher will find that children develop many independent learning skills as they form their own answers to this type of question.

- *Complex questions* are those that require complex explanations. These are still excellent questions to follow up on, but a teacher will need to think more carefully about them. They may require several sequential experiences that are then connected before the children can form their own answer. The teacher may need to divide the question into several smaller questions or provide opportunities for lengthy discussions with adults and experts.

For teachers of very young children, it is most helpful to think of *inquiry* and *complex questions* as opportunities for deep investigation. These questions are the most promising for guiding deep project work with young children.

Categorizing questions can help the teacher decide what to do next when facilitating the project. Project questions can be sorted into categories, and teachers can use these categories in deciding the most productive next steps in the project. Figure 5.2 shows the Spider Project's working project board with the children's questions grouped by categories. Children helped sort the questions. Not all questions are of equal value in terms of their contribution to deep learning, and they do not receive equal time and resources when planning for deep project work. The first response of many teachers new to project work is to find someone who will answer the children's questions or find a secondary resource such as a book or video that will have the answers. An expert, a book, or a website will usually enable children to answer these questions quickly. Using books and videos and interacting with adults are all valuable experiences; however, sometimes these can turn into

Figure 5.2. In the Spider Project, Amber helped the children sort their questions into the categories of babies, seasons, food, water, body, and home, and post them on the project board. Children added more questions as the project progressed.

passive experiences where children are primarily absorbing what others have learned. When children's questions turn into a "speaking outline for experts," it reduces project work to transmission-of-knowledge experiences. These experiences focus on the lower level of Bloom's taxonomy—*remembering, understanding,* and *applying.* These are important learning experiences for children. However, if that is the only way children answer questions, then the power of the children's questions for building mind and brain capacity is reduced, and the project lacks depth. There are many other ways that children can get their questions answered. When a teacher takes the time to analyze the questions and plan experiences that maximize active learning, then projects become more engaging and more productive for children.

Use Question Categories

Separating questions by copying them onto paper strips or sticky-notes facilitates sorting and grouping. Questions can then be grouped by type of question. The goal is not to correctly label each question, as if one is doing research, but to enable teachers to find those questions that will provide direction in project planning. Teachers should be looking for questions that are most likely to develop deep productive project experiences. The list of Spider Project questions above includes many questions that can be categorized as *fact questions*. This means that the children will need to have someone that they can ask for answers. Books and posters with photos can help children become independent in finding answers to factual questions such as the question, "Do spiders have ears?" The answer to that question is no. However, as research has shown is often the case, adults are not likely to stop with no, but to respond to what they interpret as a more complex question (Chouinard, 2007). The adult assumes that the child is wondering *how* spiders hear and may go on to explain that spiders do not have ears but they do have hairs that are extremely sensitive to air movements and they can feel sound vibrations. In this way the adult supports the growth of questioning skills at the same time that the child's knowledge base is expanded. This is another benefit of having children interact with adult experts when searching for information.

Some of the questions, especially those that begin with "How," will provide opportunities for children to investigate on their own and find the answers by observing spiders. The teacher can facilitate that by finding spiders in their natural habitat and providing an opportunity for children to watch them. The children could do observational drawings, or photograph or videotape what they see. She might also have experts bring spiders in and perhaps feed them while the children watch. She might also explore the possibility of adding a spider in an aquarium to the classroom for the duration of the project. Some of these experiences did occur in the Spider Project. Amber also found videos on the Internet of spiders making webs, creating egg sacks, moving, and eating. Although not as helpful as watching real spiders, the children were able to see them move and eat. These learning experiences enable children to use their senses and form their own answers to some of their questions.

Yet other investigation questions will require more complex answers. An example of a question that will require a more complex answer is, "Where do spiders go in the fall?" This question is an opportunity for children to hypothesize and come up with their own theories. The teacher might follow up by asking the children, "What changes occur in the fall in the place that spiders live? Will there be spiders in the snow? Where do you think spiders might go?" The teacher can write down their ideas and make a prediction chart. Even if the final answer requires expert input, children will have experienced higher-level thinking and learned that they can come up with their own answers. Children can share their ideas and what they think with an expert before the expert answers their questions.

Recognize That a Big Question Can Guide a Project

Sometimes a complex question such as "Where do spiders go in the fall?" can become a major focus of a project. That is what happened in the Pumpkin Project in Clarese Ornstein's kindergarten classroom. It was fall and across the country children were cutting open pumpkins and scooping out seeds. These experiences also happened in Clarisse's classroom, but the most enthusiastic and focused conversations were not about how gross the insides were, how many seeds were in a pumpkin, or what kind of face to carve. Instead, the children had a big question they were trying to answer: "What is happening to Mr. Weber's pumpkins?" The children had many typical questions about pumpkins, and they visited a farm, saw pumpkins of many colors, and learned how to bake pumpkin pies. These were exciting experiences for the children, but they became most excited about a mystery they discovered. Mrs. Weber, who is an assistant in the classroom, brought in a photo of her husband's garden and explained the problem that he was having. Something was eating Mr. Weber's pumpkins at night. There were pumpkins with some kind of bite marks on them. The children hypothesized a list of possible culprits and gradually eliminated animals through research and discussions with experts until they had narrowed the list of culprits to five (see Figure 5.3).

Figure 5.3. The kindergarten children narrowed down their list of animals that might be eating Mr. Weber's pumpkins.

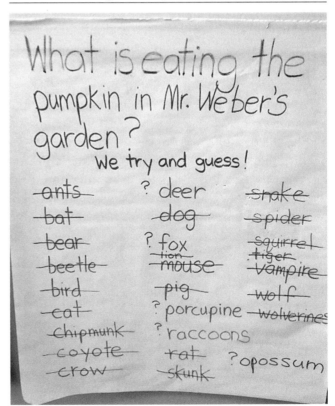

The children eliminated bears from the list when a naturalist expert explained that it would have to be an animal that lived in the area and bears did not live in Illinois. They used an iPad and follow-up conversations with experts to find out which animals eat pumpkins. The children narrowed the list to porcupine, raccoon, fox, opossum, and deer. Here are their thoughts and how they gathered the information that they wrote on the chart paper:

We see bears eating a pumpkin at a zoo. (with iPad)
We watch a porcupine eating a pumpkin. (with iPad)
Wolverines live in Canada, Alaska, and Michigan. (iPad application)
Big cats eat and play with pumpkins at zoos. (with iPad)
Lions live on savannahs. (Wyatt's information)
Tigers live in jungles, not woods. (Kaylee's information)
Many animals eat pumpkins at Richardson's Farms. (Farmer Ryan)
Wolves and bears do not live in Lake County. (Lake County Forest Preserve Educator)

The children continued to think about the pumpkin mystery outside of class, which is an indication that they were emotionally involved and the project had become meaningful to them. Clarese wrote in her Project Planning Journal that a child reported to her that when the child was eating an apple, she thought, "My apple's skin is much easier to bite than a pumpkin's skin." Another child reported that he was talking to his mother about the pumpkin mystery and asked her who she thought was eating the pumpkin. Clarese helped them summarize what they had learned and recorded their thoughts as a list of clues.

Clue 1: The animal must hide in the woods near Mr. Weber's garden.
Clue 2: The animal takes big bites out of the pumpkin.
Clue 3: The animal is not a carnivore.
Clue 4: Mr. Weber's garden is in Lake County, Illinois.

The children then had an idea that they might be able to figure out what kind of animal it was by looking at the bite marks on the pumpkin. They studied the teeth of animals left on their list by looking in books and on the Internet for photos of animals and their teeth. They observed that some had sharp teeth and some had flat teeth. Finding implements that they thought might simulate sharp and flat teeth (a fork and pant-hanger clips), they proceeded with their experiment (see Figure 5.4).

The children thought that the pant-hanger clip made marks more like those in the pumpkins in Mr. Weber's garden. When Clarese shared the children's progress with other teachers, one of them suggested that they might try to borrow a night vision wildlife camera which they could set up in Mr. Weber's garden at night. This was very exciting. They were able to borrow a camera, and the children were able to confirm that the culprit was

Figure 5.4. These kindergarten children are using a fork to simulate sharp-toothed animals in their quest to find out who is eating Mr. Weber's pumpkins.

a deer. The project did not end there. The children were interested in how a farmer might protect the pumpkins from animals. They learned from Farmer Ryan ways that they protect their pumpkins. The project ended when the children constructed a scarecrow for Mr. Weber, and the children made a book entitled, "Who is Eating Mr. Weber's Pumpkins? A Kindergarten Investigation."

The pumpkin mystery is a good example of how a teacher can extend and deepen project work by allowing children time to think and to form their own ideas rather than relying on an expert for a quick answer. It is also an excellent example of how a teacher can effectively use technology to enrich, not overwhelm, children's investigations.

Collect and Record Questions

When collecting questions from children, teachers find it helpful to post them in the classroom. Even in projects with toddlers, posting of questions helps keep the focus on what children are thinking, even if they are only read by the adults in the room. Questions may be collected during a webbing discussion or they may be collected while making a list. Of course, questions are written down as they occur spontaneously or are observed, but at some point in projects of preschoolers and older children, it is helpful for the teacher to sit down with children and formally make a list or web of their questions. Sometimes teachers record them with the names of children who asked them. This is helpful when grouping children or forming committees. Questions are also often put on cards or sticky notes so they can be arranged into webs or lists as Amber did on the project board shown in Figure 5.2. This enables the teacher to see areas of greatest interest or to put into categories for deciding next steps in a project.

Challenging children to think of possible answers or to predict which answer is correct is an easy way to provide opportunities for children to practice higher-level thinking skills. These can be recorded next to a child-generated question. That is what happened in Nick Pettit's 2nd-grade classroom at Scuola Vita Nuova Charter School in Kansas City, Missouri, when they did the Cliff Drive Nature

Project. They investigated Cliff Drive, a corridor of natural features unique to the Missouri River Valley including limestone bluffs, natural vegetation, and wildlife. Cliff Dive is particularly unusual because it is located immediately adjacent to the city core, which is a heavily urbanized environment. Cliff Drive is located less than one mile from the school. Nick's 2nd-graders were very interested in the nature corridor, and some of them did not know about it before the project began. The 2nd-graders organized into groups according to their interests: the Rock Group, the Plants and Trees Group, and the Cliff Group. The children developed questions related to their topic and then found the answers to their questions. When Nick talked with the groups, he recorded their questions, their predictions, their answers, and also the sources for their answers as the project progressed. This focus on questions empowered the students to direct their learning and to communicate to the rest of the class what they had learned. Figure 5.5 shows Nick's chart for the Cliff Group on his classroom wall.

The chart from the project work of the Cliff Group shows not only how the students found the answers to their questions but also how the students in Nick's class were able to develop some

Figure 5.5. On this chart of questions, the Cliff Group 2nd-grade committee recorded predicted answers, actual answers, and how they found out the information.

of the specific skills that they needed according to Grade 2 Common Core State Standards. The following standards were covered in the Cliff Project:

- Participate in collaborative conversations with diverse partners about grade 2 topics and texts with peers and adults in small and larger groups.
- Follow agreed-upon rules for discussions (e.g., gaining the floor in respectful ways, listening to others with care, speaking one at a time about the topics and texts under discussion).
- Build on others' talk in conversations by linking their comments to the remarks of others.
- Ask for clarification and further explanation as needed about the topics and texts under discussion.
- Recount or describe key ideas or details from a text read aloud or information presented orally or through other media.
- Ask and answer questions about what a speaker says in order to clarify comprehension, gather additional information, or deepen understanding of a topic or issue.

ASKING TEACHER'S PROJECT QUESTIONS

Question asking in project work isn't limited to children's questions. Teachers can and should ask their own questions because they are modeling intellectual curiosity for their children. When a teacher finds out an answer to his question, the teacher's reaction to this is often genuine satisfaction. Sometimes teachers hesitate to offer questions because they think they are taking over the children's project. Generally, this is an addition to the project and will often spark additional children's questions.

Most questions of teachers in project work, however, are directed at children to foster and deepen their thinking about their project work. There are some general guidelines that can be applied not just in project work but in all meaningful interactions with children. These emphasize building awareness within children of their own thinking, that metacognition referred to in MBE Instructional Guideline 9. Dombro, Jablon, and Stetson (2011) suggest focusing on thinking in conversations with children. Strategies include using the words *think* and *thinking* as you talk with children, using a gesture to indicate thinking such as pointing to your forehead, preparing children by telling them you are going to ask a question, telling children that you notice they are thinking, and giving children time to think after you ask a question.

Some teachers new to project work have difficulty coming up with questions that will challenge children to think or extend their learning, so opportunities for deeper project work are missed. This is especially true of projects in classrooms of very young children where much of teacher thinking occurs on the fly, or in the process of overseeing a very busy classroom. The opportunity to ask a challenging question may pass very quickly as children move from one activity to the next. Bloom's taxonomy, especially the new revised taxonomy of the cognitive domain (Marzano & Kendall, 2006), can be helpful as a framework for generating questions to ask children. The revised hierarchy is focused on what children *do*, which makes it easier to apply to project work. For example, previously the first level was *knowledge*. In the revised hierarchy, the first level is *remembering*. A teacher can think, "What can I ask to get the child to *remember* during this project?" Questions might include, "What did the farmer feed the chickens?" or "Can you tell me the names of the different animals we saw?" The result of the question is that the child *remembers* and responds. Pohl (2000) provides ideas on how the taxonomy can be used to generate questions that help children learn how to think. In the list below I have adapted some of his questions for project work with young children. They are presented as stems to questions; that is, they are examples of how to begin a question. The teacher can complete the rest of the questions using the content of the project. The questions have also been adapted for young children.

Questions for Remembering

What happened after . . . ?
How many . . . ?
What is . . . ?
Who was it that . . . ?
Can you name . . . ?
Who spoke to . . . ?
Which is true or false . . . ?

Questions for Understanding

Can you tell why . . . ?
How would you tell somebody . . . ?
Can you tell me step by step how . . . ?
First what happened? Then what happened next?
What do you think could have happened next . . . ?
Who do you think . . . ?
Can you tell me more about that so I understand it?
Can you draw that so I understand?

Questions for Applying

Do you know of another time (place) where . . . ?
Can you put these things together such as . . . ?
   (Group by characteristics)
What would change if . . . ?
What questions would you ask of . . . ?
Could you tell someone else how to . . . . .?

Question for Analyzing

How is . . . the same as . . . ?
How is . . . different from . . . ?
Why did . . . changes occur?
What do you think must have happened when . . . ?
What are some of the problems with . . . ?
Can you tell me the differences between . . . ?
What was the problem with . . . ?

Questions for Evaluating

Can you think of a better way to . . . ?
Do you think . . . is a good or bad thing? Why?
What changes to . . . would you suggest?
Do you believe . . . ? How would you feel if . . . ?
Do you think . . . is working the way it should?
What are the other ways (or ideas) for . . . ?

Questions for Creating

Can you design a . . . to . . . ?
Can you see a way to fix the problem?
If you had anything you needed, how would you . . . ?
Why don't you make up your own way to . . . ?
What would happen if . . . ?

Teachers often put this list on a clipboard or on the wall, to remind themselves of how they might ask more meaningful and productive questions.

SOME FINAL QUESTIONS

Asking questions, as we learned in the beginning of this chapter, is a natural way that children, indeed all of us, find things out. Even toddlers let us know when they have a question, so having schools focused on questions should be natural. However, based on my experience, that is not happening. My question is, why not? More often I see a lack of opportunities for children to ask questions—questions go unheard and "unasked." I had a professor who always said there are no dumb questions. I agree. Here are some last questions: Why should anyone think a question is dumb? Or judge a person for asking a question? Or fear to ask a question in school? That is something we educators should be able to fix.

CHAPTER 6

Representing Thought

Representations are an important part of the project approach. When engaged in project work, children represent their ideas in a variety of ways. They create drawings, paintings, block structures, models, play environments, sculptures, songs, stories, books, and a myriad of other expressions of their thought processes. These expressions are commonly referred to as *representations*. I like to use the term *render* when talking with teachers about representation. Render commonly means to melt down or to extract. In project representation, children extract what they have learned about a topic and bring it forth, to communicate it. Rendering takes work, lots of mental work. For a representation to be a rendering, it must come from the child's mind. It must be the child's idea.

TO RENDER AN IDEA— A CHILD'S OR THE TEACHER'S?

Loris Malaguzzi of the schools of Reggio Emilia, Italy, often talked about the diverse outpouring from young children's minds, described in the poem "The Hundred Languages of Children" (quoted in Edwards et al., 1993). These "languages" provide evidence and insight into the inner world of children's thoughts and remind us that children have many, many languages that they use to understand and to speak. It is through these many languages of children that we can see what children wonder about, what ideas they have, and what they are learning. There is, of course, no numbered list of 100 ways children do this, but the number is symbolic of the richness of the world of the child. Calling these learning experiences languages is especially appropriate because languages are systems that people devise to communicate their thoughts and feelings to each other. When we use a language, we are articulating our thoughts and feelings. To use a language, we have to learn the structure and rules of that language and how to form and transform our expressions into meaningful communication. As in all language use, the act of learning the language supports the building of mind and brain capacity of children.

In the project approach the variety of languages of children is respected, and they are encouraged to express themselves in many ways. In classrooms where deep project work is occurring, I have found that children not only use a number of languages to express their thoughts but also use these languages to grapple with or think through ideas as they create their representations. They discuss building and construction problems with other children in the process of creating classroom–community-designed representations. The Seed Store in Michelle's classroom described in Chapter 1 is an example of how children work together to build a common vision in their representations. Their Seed Store is a representation of the Kelly Seed Store in Peoria, Illinois. In the process of constructing their own seed store, first the children had to *think* about all that they knew about the real store, including the bins, the scales, the cash register, and the important seed-mixing machine.

Representations and the process of representing often differentiate project work from thematic teaching and teacher-directed inquiry approaches. Figure 6.1 is a representation of a spider using a paper plate. This is a common teacher-directed activity, which appears in many thematic units on spiders. The paper-plate spider is the kind of learning experience that often appears in commercial curriculum guides as a suggested art activity to accompany a thematic unit. It is supposed to represent a spider. The paper-plate spider is, basically, a craft activity that is then labeled "spider." It could just as easily be labeled octopus because there is little resemblance to a real spider. Many teachers, parents, and administrators see no harm in this type of activity and may even find the dangling spiders "charming" or "cute." However, when the thinking processes required to create the paper-plate spider are analyzed, the activity appears less harmless. Although some say this craft has different goals, especially goals of following directions and practicing fine motor control, creating paper-plate spiders under teacher direction conforms to very few of the instructional guidelines of MBE Science (see Chapter 1). Making paper-plate spiders is unlikely to create an environment for intellectual conversations (MBE Science Instructional Guideline 1) and has limited sense and meaning for children (MBE Science Instructional Guideline 2). It fails to link real content knowledge about spiders to the process, and could not be described as active learning (MBE

Science Instructional Guideline 8). Some adults describe this as active learning since children are gluing and folding, but active learning includes an active mind. "Hands-on" does not necessarily mean that children's minds are also "on." This activity requires little higher-level thinking by children. Although technically harmless, these types of experiences take time out of a school day that may already be packed with teacher-directed and -determined content and provide little opportunity for children to think and to process what they are learning in their own way or using their own "language." There is also considerable danger that such activities discourage children from doing the hard work of making their own representation. When representation tasks are taken over by the teacher, they cease to come from within the children. It becomes a representation not of what is in children's minds but what is in the teacher's mind. The teacher has made many choices in the process of planning and preparing this experience. Each choice made has taken a choice away from the children. Some of the teacher's choices in the paper-plate spider representation include the following:

Figure 6.1. This paper plate spider has little similarity to a real spider, fails to provoke thought, and teaches misconceptions about spiders.

- *Choice of Materials*—The teacher selected the materials to be used in the representation, and the materials shaped the representation. For example, common spider colors include black, brown, orange, yellow, green, and white, but the teacher provided only black paint.
- *Choice of Spider*—Even though there are a variety of kinds of spiders with a variety of body shapes and leg types, by selecting the paper plate, the teacher has limited the spider choice to those spiders with large round abdomens. In fact, spiders have two body parts.
- *Choice of Leg Construction*—By choosing to create legs as dangling accordion folded paper, the teacher has deprived children of the opportunity to think about the real structure of spider legs. Spiders have eight legs with seven segments with a claw at the end of each leg. This choice eliminated the opportunity to solve the problem of how to create a segmented leg with a claw.

- *Choice of Google Eyes*—By choosing commercial wiggle eyes for the children, the teacher has not only taken away choice but has also taught a misconception. Spiders usually have eight eyes, some six or less. These eyes are not similar to the human eye. There are many different types of eyes including searchlight and reflector eyes. The differences are related to how and when the spiders hunt.

The paper-plate spider is also not authentic, as I have indicated in the list above. These choices made by the teacher lowered the intellectual level of conversation and problem solving. As you read the critique of the teacher decisions listed above, you may have found yourself becoming curious and engaged as you learned some things you did not know about spiders. If these choices had been made by the children instead of the teacher, the activity would have not only been more engaging and more joyful for children but also enhanced their mind and brain capacity.

Unfortunately this type of art activity often appears in "project work" or "studies" when teachers are focused more on products than on what children are thinking and learning. I observed a similar paper-plate spider in documentation of a learning experience that the teacher described as project work. It is often the representations by children that reveal whether a study is a project or a theme and whether or not the experience is on the right side or the left side of the continuum of child-initiated and child-directed experiences as described in Chapter 2. The paper-plate spider is an extreme example of teacher direction in project work and more typical of thematic units. Most teachers facilitating project work do involve children in the decision-making process. Fewer decisions are made by the teacher and more by the children. However, I have seen many representations such as cardboard school buses, models, and art products such as murals that appear to be designed by adults. A simple way to increase the depth and effectiveness of project work is to let children do more of the decision making in the representation process.

THE SPIDER PROJECT: AN EXAMPLE

In contrast to the paper-plate spider learning experience, what would happen if children were empowered to make the decisions in representation? What would that look like? This can be seen in the Spider Project in Amber Forrest's class of 4-year-olds introduced in Chapter 5. Although this is a pre-K class, the facilitation that Amber provided is appropriate for guiding projects in kindergarten and early primary grades also. At the older ages, children would be able to do even more of their own research and have a greater repertoire of ways to represent than these 4-year-olds.

Recall that the Spider Project began when the children discovered a daddy longlegs in the playhouse on the playground. When Amber shared information with her class that daddy longlegs weren't really spiders, the children asked, "What makes a spider?" Amber knew this would be a powerful topic because she observed that all of the children were engaged and motivated. From the beginning of the project, she saw the topic had potential for significant growth in knowledge and skills because investigating spiders would naturally cover many literacy, math, cognitive, and science goals and objectives. There were many significant events that occurred in the project process, including frequent field site visits (hikes) around the property of the preschool where the children could observe a variety of spiders. Amber also arranged to have a naturalist for Polk County Conservation, Miss Patty, come and answer initial questions. Another expert, Mr. Mike, from Aqualand Pet Store, spent a morning in the classroom. He brought spiders, including a large tarantula, to the classroom, answered children's questions, and had extended conversations with individual and small groups of children (see Figure 6.2).

Observational Drawing

The children created extensive observational drawings during field site visits and during Mr. Mike's visit (MBE Science Instructional Guideline 8); see Figure 6.3. These became the children's

Figure 6.2. Mr. Mike, a visiting expert, showed his pet tarantula. This very exciting experience for children inspired many drawings and other representations.

Figure 6.3. Ben's Observational Drawing of Mr. Mike's Tarantula

notes. Amber uses observational drawing as a strategy to help the children notice details in objects and to capture phenomena. In the drawings of spiders, children included details such as the pedipalps and spinnerets. She also used observational drawing to refresh the children's memory (MBE Science Instructional Guideline 3) and for children to discuss what they had learned (MBE Science Instructional Guideline 9). For example, children referred to their initial spider drawings when later creating their three-dimensional spider representations.

Children continued to study spiders outside. Amber placed books and other research material in a basket that the children carried outside for

immediate access for research as they observed spiders (see Figure 6.4). Children continued observational drawing of the spiders and webs they found. They used what they were learning in their drawing (see Figure 6.5). Amber describes observational drawing in the project this way:

> Observation drawing came very naturally. We had not really taught observation drawing yet so we had to take some time to teach them how to do that—how to observe something, how to look at it, and how to put what they see on paper. I had to do my own drawing so I could think what I would notice about this object so I did a lot of my own drawing in this project. I could see how they progressed in the details that they would add. I loved it when they would be sitting down and they had drawn a lot. Then I would sit down by them and see what they had drawn, such as the legs. I would say, "You know, did you notice the legs here? Are they straight or do they have connections?" So then they noticed that the legs have a joint. Some spiders have two joints, some have four. Then I would see them make the leg so it would bend in those certain joints. Not every child, of course, noticed these things and incorporated them in their drawings, but many of them would think about our conversation and then incorporate it into their drawings. I would just try to encourage them by really looking at their work and looking at the object with the child and having a conversation about their work. They would say things like, "Oh, this one has hairs on it!" Then pretty soon little hairs started showing up on the drawing. I just take the time to connect with each child and help them notice the different parts, not tell them how to draw it but more how to look closely and think about it. Learning to look at things closely is important, just like looking at letters; you have to notice the different parts.

Children also incorporated these observed details into their play, creating a web on the playground fence and pretending to be a spider in the play area (see Figure 6.6). Another child learning about a spider egg sac found an egg carton, put little black things in it, and taped it up to make a representation of an egg sac. She connected the egg carton with the egg sac. Although there was some painting in this project, observing real spiders and their webs and drawing what they

Figure 6.4. Andrew and Peyton use books to learn about spinnerets.

Figure 6.5. Andrew and Ben create observational drawings of the tangled webs they found.

observed was the primary activity during Phase II investigation.

The Spider Museum

Eventually the children began to get all of their questions answered and became less interested in finding and drawing spiders and webs. Amber then initiated a class discussion about how they might share what they have learned with others. She shared with them some ways other children in other projects have shared their work. One child said he wanted to make a certain kind of spider and show it to someone. Then another child said he could make a different kind of spider, and then everybody started telling the kind of spider they would want to make. Then a child said, "Let's all make a spider!" Amber introduced the idea of putting all their spiders together like a museum for others to see. That idea was very exciting to the children, and they decided that they would create a spider museum. Ben immediately made a sign for the museum.

Each child created a representation for the museum. The photos of the children's work for the Spider Museum are included in a full-color insert. As you view the photos of their work, refer to Figure 6.7 to read about how individual children approached this task and created their representations.

Figure 6.6. Even the playground became an area for spider project work. Children are creating a variety of webs with yarn.

Abby

Addy

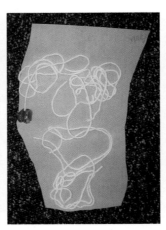
Anna

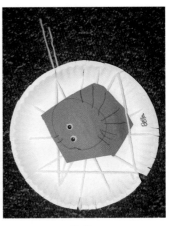
Bella

Ben

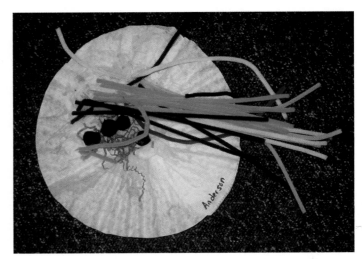
Anderson

Andrew's Drawing

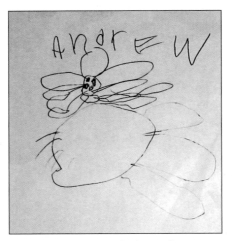
Andrew's Plan for his Sculpture

Andrew's Sculpture

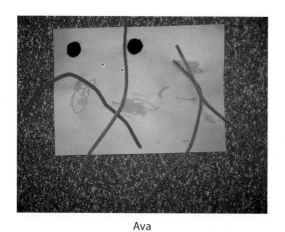

Ava

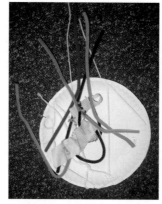

Cael

Gehrig

Gabe

Drew

Jacob

Brolen

Chance

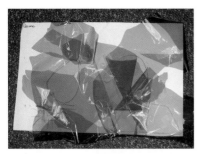

Jaime

Kevin

Mia

Lane

Laney

Luke S. and Josie

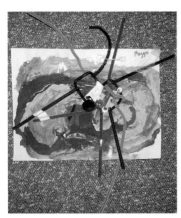

Maggie

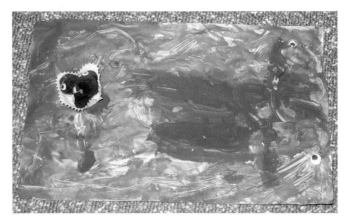

DeDe

Josh

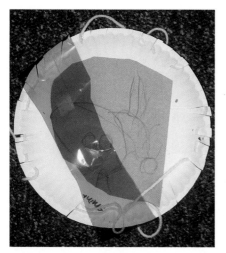

Shaina

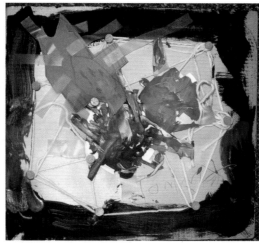

Tommy

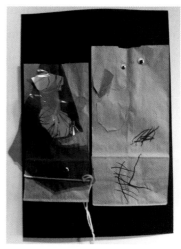

Luke L.

Lucy

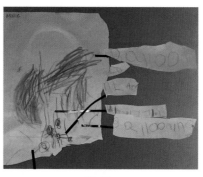

Mollie

Peyton

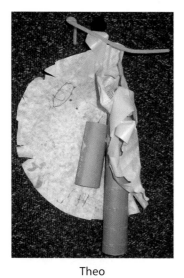

Theo

Sam H.

Sam S.

Figure 6.7. The representations in the Spider Museum reveal each child's knowledge about spiders and each child's individual approach to the representation challenge.

Name	Description of Representation Process
Abby	Abby planned to use pipe cleaners. However, as she was manipulating them she found that they would not bend in the way in which she intended. After a couple of days' work she twirled them around her fingers to make the body and the remaining pieces became the legs.
Addy *Wolf spider with egg sac*	Addy was very interested in the mother spider and her egg sac. She knew that this spider had more than two eyes, which she demonstrated using pieces of a paper plate. To make the egg sacs she used mini muffin liners and pom-pom balls.
Anderson	Anderson joined the class almost at the end of the spider project. He did not have a lot of knowledge or experience with spiders. He knew that they had a lot of legs. He chose to have his spider on an alien ship.
Andrew *Wolf spider*	Andrew had been fascinated with the wolf spider for much of the project. He had created many observational drawings from pictures in books. He decided to use clay for his medium. He sculpted legs, spinnerets, pedipalps, and two body parts.
Anna *Tarantula*	Anna wanted to create a tarantula and show how it uses its web to return back to its home because its vision is not very good.
Ava	Ava had joined us halfway through the project. She knew that spiders had legs and some spiders had a set of small eyes and a set of large eyes.
Beth *Red spider*	Beth wanted her spider in a web. Her idea spread to others and others began to add webs to their spiders.
Ben *Wolf spider*	Ben would much rather draw a spider. He is able to create observational drawings with extreme detail. However, making a construction is more challenging. He took his construction apart several times and put it back together.
Brolen *Baby spider with parachute web*	Brolen was very impressed that baby spiders left their place of birth by flying. They create their own parachutes out of web to catch the wind. He wanted his parachute to really work. He found that just yarn wouldn't work; he had to have something to catch the air, so he decided on a paper plate.
Cael	Cael wanted his spider to stick inside the web. He tried glue over and over again. He couldn't get the pipe cleaners to stick. He figured out the tape would work best.
Chance	Chance began by painting an entire piece of paper black. Then he knew that spiders were round so he cut a circle. To add legs he taped on pipe cleaners. He tried to tape all at once and realized when he pulled the tape off to fix something that it took the paint with it. He finished the spider by using small pieces of tape for each leg.
DeDe *Wolf spider*	DeDe discovered that Addy used pom-pom balls for baby spiders and thought that was a good idea. She decided that the babies needed eyes as well.
Drew	Drew wanted to make a big spider. He had several problems he solved including counting the pipe cleaners, attaching the legs, and learning how to hold the eyes until the glue set up. Drew displayed persistence and problem solving.
Gabe *Jumping spider*	Gabe saw a picture of a spider jumping onto a flower in a book. The abdomen was very large and the head small. The spider also was carrying babies on her back. Gabe wanted the legs to look like they were in the book, pushing back in a jumping motion. He also created the flower for the spider to jump on.
Gehrig	Gehrig wanted his spider to have big eyes. He used a wood block and nails to make his web—similar to an activity done earlier in the project.
Jacob	Jacob spent his time away from the rest of his classmates. He worked on his project with little discussion with other students or teacher. He remembered that some spiders had hair on them. The yellow pieces are the spider's hairs.
Jaime *Water spider*	Jaime wanted to show the air pocket water spiders make for their egg sacs under water. He drew a picture and used blue cellophane to represent the water.

Figure 6.7 (continued). The representations in the Spider Museum reveal each child's knowledge about spiders and each child's individual approach to the representation challenge.

Name	Description of Representation Process
Josh	Josh cut an egg carton into many small pieces first, then used pieces for the body and legs. He later added pipe cleaners for legs. Then he added a pom-pom ball for the head.
Kevin *Trap door spider*	Kevin saw an observational drawing that Brolen did of a trap door spider. He decided to create the hole using papier-mâché. He created the spider out of clay. He added several legs and the pedipalps on the head.
Lane *Tarantula*	This was the first time Lane had used clay. He practiced for several days creating the snakes to make legs. He didn't want to get rid of any of them so he used all the snakes he had created on the spider.
Laney *Ground sac spider*	Laney saw this spider on the cover of a book. She began by cutting out construction paper for the different colors and then drew the rest. She found that the legs on this spider had tiny little hairs. She also wanted to label the parts of the spider like an activity we had done previously in the project.
Lucy	Lucy created her spider out of clay. She had an exact plan—body and eight legs, which she accomplished in one day, and two eyes, which she added the next day. After that she proceeded to help others with their spiders.
Luke L.	He created his spider and web out of lunch sacks. He wanted to show that the spider attaches to the web with more webbing.
Luke S. and Josie *Tarantula*	Luke S. and Josie were the only two who chose to do their spider together. They created their spider out of papier-mâché. They divided the work between them. One made the head and the other the body. They disagreed on the color of the legs at first but then decided to make them different on each side.
Maggie	Maggie began by painting a web. As she was creating it, she told me that webs circle around and around. She was able to twist the pipe cleaners around each other to make the spider stay together.
Mia	Mia told me that she had seen spider webs made on paper plates and that is what she wanted to do. She drew the spider first on the paper plate and then put yarn on it. It wouldn't stay on the plate. She figured out how to make slits. Mia first made seven legs. Later she realized there were only seven and quickly added one more.
Mollie *Spiderlings*	Mollie had been very excited about the baby spiders for much of the project. She decided that she wanted to make a big poster showing how the spiderlings left their place of birth, also called ballooning.
Peyton	Peyton made a drawing of a spider, then painted it. He wanted to show how the web came out of the back of the spider.
Sam S.	Sam S. twisted pipe cleaners around to create the body and legs of the spider. However, when it came to putting them together he struggled. He proceeded to tape them together.
Sam H. *Water spider*	Sam H. wanted his spider to be on a web and inside a bubble. He also drew several eyes in different sizes on his spider. He borrowed the idea of the cellophane from Shaina.
Shaina *Water spider*	Shaina wanted her spider to swim in the water. She drew a picture of a spider and attached it to a web. Then she just wanted to add a little water so the spider could breathe, so she chose cellophane to represent water.
Theo	Theo started with a large coffee filter. He decided to make the legs using masking tape. As he worked for several days, he realized that the legs made of tape kept sticking together. He wrapped the coffee filter around a paper towel tube. This separated the legs and made them stand apart. Then he added a pipe cleaner for the pedipalps.
Tommy *Spider and the enemy*	Every observational drawing that Tommy did always included a bug (enemy) that the spider would eat. He made a web using a piece of cardboard and yarn. He cut out shapes and glued them together to make the spider and the enemy caught in the web.

The creation of the Spider Museum is an excellent example of MBE Science Instructional Guideline 7: Orchestrated Immersion. The teacher "immerses students in complex experiences that support learning by calling on individuals one by one to bring out their voices and then weaving them into a single class experience" (Tokuhama-Espinosa, 2010, p. 121). The children were motivated to create their representation and had to remember what they had learned in their investigation to create their spider (MBE Science Instructional Guideline 3). Students were active and displayed higher-order thinking skills as they created a vision of what they wanted to make and then followed through, making that vision a reality (MBE Science Instructional Guideline 8).

Problem solving occurred frequently in this spider representation process. The creation of a spider for the museum required that each child set a goal, follow through, strive to solve problems, and persist, all indicators of the development of executive function skills, as described in Chapter 2. For example, Drew faced and overcame a number of difficulties in the creation of his spider. Amber describes his experience:

> Drew wanted to make a big spider. After he had painted the body, he recognized he needed legs. It was a challenge for him to count enough pipe cleaners for the spider. The pipe cleaners moved around so easily when he touched them causing him to double count. He solved that problem by putting them in a line and being extra careful to only point at them without touching to count. Then he wanted to attach the legs to the spider but he didn't want the tape to show so he used clear tape. This created a problem because taping each leg side by side was a challenge. He became frustrated because he couldn't get the legs in the right position and when he rearranged them they pulled off the paint. He sought help with his problem, saying, "I can't do it." He was able to tell Mrs. Johnson what the problem was, and she helped him come up with several possible ways to solve the problem including putting several legs together on one strip of tape. When he began putting the eyes on, the glue kept running, and the eyes kept falling off. After several attempts at different solutions, he figured out by himself that holding the eye for a little while would make it stay. Drew was persistent and purposeful in his work and enormously satisfied when he got his spider to look just the way he wanted it.

Drew's work is also a good example of executive function—hill, skill, and will (Moran & Gardner, 2010). Drew had a clear goal in mind, he had to develop skills to make it happen, and he had to be committed to working it out and following through. Representation opportunities such as the creation of the Spider Museum enable children to experience what it is like to set their own goals and stick to them even though the work can be hard. Drew also learned that he can get help when he needs it and that adults will be willing to let him still control his own project.

The Spider Museum is also an excellent example of how a representation opportunity can enable children to use content learned in a meaningful, authentic way. This was a powerful learning experience for these children. They were able to use the content that they had learned, engage in processes that were appropriate for that content, and create a meaningful product. Katz (2003) advocates increasing the overlap of these three components in project work to maximize intellectual development (see Figure 6.8).

The representation experiences of the paper-plate spider and the Spider Museum are compared in Figure 6.9 using the generic Katz diagram (shown in Figure 6.8). The children's understanding of *content* (definition of a spider, the parts of the spider, and what each part does) is not necessary in the paper-plate spider activity, nor is the spider's relationship to its web. The *process* required by children to make the product is one of following directions and copying. The process of creating the product required neither an analysis of the spider and its parts nor a decision about what material would be best to create it (e.g., the jointed leg). The *products* are contrived and inauthentic. In contrast,

Figure 6.8. Increasing the overlap of the quality of processes, products, and content in project work maximizes intellectual development.

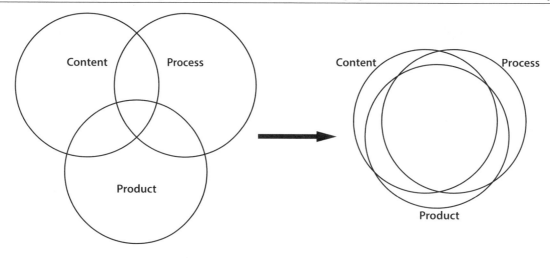

Source: Katz, 2003, p. 17.

the spiders in the Spider Museum were built after careful analysis of real spiders *(content)*. The *process* involved children reviewing their observations and thinking about what they had learned in their study of real spiders and how to incorporate that into their representations. The *products* are representations that have many characteristics of a real spider and provide evidence of what the children have learned. The products are rich in both content and higher-level thinking experiences.

Amber's Role as Facilitator

It might be helpful to learn about the decisions that Amber made in facilitating the Spider Project,

in "orchestrating" this experience. Here she describes her thoughts and experiences:

As soon as the children said that they each wanted to make their own spider, I decided that I would let them use whatever material they wanted as long as they told me what they wanted. That was a big decision for me to make. After I said that, I wasn't sure at first that it was a good idea. The other teachers thought I was crazy and predicted pandemonium in the classroom. This is how I managed it. We always start with a circle time before our center time, which is a child-selection period of the day. The first

Figure 6.9. How effective is the product as a representation of the content and processes that the children learned about?

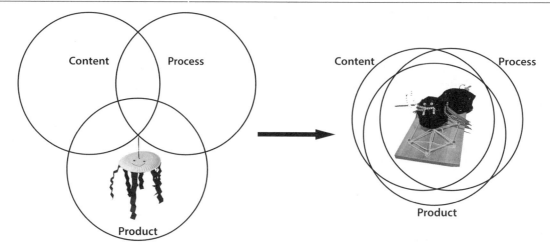

morning I took a few of the children at a time. I reminded them that we had decided in the group to make a spider museum and the group had decided that each child should make a spider of his or her choice, a spider that they had learned about. Then each child told me what kind of spider he or she would work on and with what materials. I had to get a few things, but mostly I just needed to point them in the right direction. From then on, every day I would write down what their plan was for that day, and they would go off and work where they wanted to. Not every child worked on his or her spider every day. Most of the time we would have children everywhere in the classroom. There were many materials being worked with all over the classroom: clay, pipe cleaners, cupcake liners, paint, and even papier-mâché.

I asked them to tell me what they were going to work on that day, exactly what part of the spider they would work on. Sometimes they knew, and sometimes they needed to look at it first. Then I asked them what kind of materials they were going to use that day and if they needed help. That helped me know if another child could help them or if it needed to be a teacher. Most of the time they would say things such as, "I am going to work on my water spider, and I need something that will look like it is under the water." Sometimes I would help them think through that decision. For example, we looked at the kinds of paper for the water spider. First Sam H. chose wax paper, but it didn't really work very well, so he ended up with blue cellophane wrap, which would look like the spider was under the water. Sometimes they needed help cutting, which we would always do, if asked. They needed some help cutting to the right size.

Two children were using papier-mâché. They did ask for help. They couldn't get it to stick to the balloon and they needed help to figure that out. They ended up making it thicker.

Another day a child started with a papier-mâché body and then decided he wanted to make a trap-door spider, a spider that is in a hole and sets a door at the top so the animal could fall in and the spider could eat it. He made the hole out of the papier-mâché and needed help cutting a door in it. He tried several times to do it himself, and it just crumbled. Then he figured out that you need to make the hole for the door first, and that worked for him.

One child wanted to make a web for his spider. He wanted to kind of make it come up from the ground. He brought a block of wood from home. He created his vision, but he wasn't happy with it; he wanted it to stand off of the wood like it was a real web, not touch the wood. He said he needed something to hold it up. We figured out you could hammer nails into the wood and then you could make the web without it touching the wood. He needed help in hammering the nails so he showed me where he wanted each nail, and I hammered it in. Then he wound it with yarn to make this real cool web and put his spider on top. The children became very proficient at using tools.

Most of the work on the museum was done during center time. I started by grouping them into small groups but that really didn't work very well. It was much easier for me to say to them, "Get the materials you need, and find a place to work." It didn't matter where it was. Not all children worked on their spider every day. They were also playing in the centers, painting, doing puzzles, and so on. I could walk around and help them if they needed it and talk to them about their work. One thing I noticed is that they did a lot of talking to each other while they were working on their spiders. Much more than when they were doing other things like puzzles. It actually ran very smoothly because the children were so engaged and so focused on what they were doing.

Gradually children began completing their spiders and then the actual display and museum opening was planned as the culminating event for the project (Phrase III of the project approach, refer to Figure 3.1). Parents, project experts, and friends were invited to the opening. Amber created four documentation panels that told the story of the Spider Project, including one entitled "The Spider Museum: A Work in Progress, Representation of Learning." Panels were placed around the room with photos and drawings of children's work, and of course, the spider representations (see Figure 6.10).

ENCOURAGING REPRESENTATION

As there are many languages of children, there are also many different kinds of representation experiences that can deepen children's project experiences. These can be effective when children make the choices and do the thinking so that they are rendering what they are learning or have learned about the topic in the representations. Some of these are listed here:

- *Oral Representations*—Stories told; presentations to parents, classrooms, or the community; guided tours of displays or play environments; plays
- *Artistic Products*—Drawings, paintings, murals, sculptures
- *Music Products*—Songs, operettas, musical performances
- *Written Representations*—Labels for charts, diagrams, child- or class-written books, posters, captions for displays, project histories
- *Play Environments*—Creation of habitats; creation of play businesses or work sites; creation of a home environment related to the topic (such as a kitchen in a cooking project)
- *Three-dimensional Models and Structures*— Constructions using recycled materials, blocks, or Legos; small models that demonstrate processes; creation of habitats; historical dioramas (2nd grade and above)
- *Data Explanation and Displays*—Posters; PowerPoint or web presentations with explanations; flow charts of processes; photograph displays with narratives

Figure 6.10. Father and son discuss his spider on display in the museum.

To be effective as learning experiences, these representations need to be expressions of what the children are thinking about the topic and what they have learned. They need to be renderings of what is in children's minds. When representations are authentic expressions of the individual child's thinking, teachers can utilize these representations to evaluate an individual child's achievement of standards and required curriculum goals. For example, in the Chicken Project in Pam Scranton's preschool classroom at Discovery Preschool in Peoria, Illinois, some of the children produced drawings of the chicken in various stages of the life cycle, from egg to baby chick to full-grown chicken. Some children created posters of the life cycle, some made models out of play dough, and some pretended to be baby chicks hatching from eggs. As they talked with Pam about their renderings, Pam was able to assess which Illinois Early Learning and Development Standard they had achieved. For example, all these children had achieved the science standard 12.A, "Understand that living things grow and change." Many also achieved standards 26.A, "Understand processes, traditional tools and modern technologies used in the arts," and 26.B, "Understand ways to express meaning through the arts." It is in the "putting out" of what they know. Unlike craft projects, books, or scripted plays that are conceived by the teacher and copied by the children in thematic units, authentic representation in project work challenges individual children to think about what they know and use it. This thinking, and the accomplishment of the goals and standards, is easily revealed and documented in their work.

An analysis of the Spider Project reveals several key decisions that Amber made that enabled the Spider Museum to be an authentic representation experience. Here are some guidelines based on her experiences and the experiences of other teachers facilitating deep project work.

Don't rush representations. Amber focused in the investigation phase on building children's knowledge and understanding of spiders and finding answers to their questions. She provided extensive time for children to visit and revisit the sites where the spiders lived and encouraged observational drawing, sketching, and play. Children's representation is an expression of what they have learned—the knowledge they have gained and the understanding of parts, relationships, and purposes. Children must have something they can think about before they can render those thoughts in the form of representations.

Keep representation goals open-ended. Amber did not have a predetermined model or a goal for what she thought the children should do. She talked with the children in a group about how they might share what they have learned and how other children have shared what they learned in other projects. She then facilitated a discussion of options, and when children were headed in the direction of the Spider Museum, she enthusiastically supported that, even though she was not sure how she would manage its creation.

Encourage children to make individual decisions. Rendering is about a child taking everything she knows and bringing it forth in some kind of product. It may be a structure, a play scenario, or a painting. It is important to remember that rendering is an individual intellectual experience requiring individuals to use their own knowledge and

understanding. It is the thinking that occurs that is most important. Each child must have an opportunity to do deep thinking in project work. Sometimes large classroom representations in project work become an intellectual experience of just a few children. Creation of large play environments or structures is most effective when there is a way for representations of individuals to be blended together to achieve a classroom goal. The idea of a museum for the spiders provided a common structure and goal even though individuals worked on their own representation. For example, creating a grocery store for the play area can involve many children creating materials, equipment, costumes, flyers, and products for the store. It is important that each child have an entry point at their appropriate level of participation. Amber respected individual children's choices in how they wanted to form their representations. When Mollie decided that she wanted to make a poster about how the spiderlings created parachutes for travel and not a model, Amber supported her work.

Support children by discussing with them what they know and what they remember about what they are observing. Before, during, and after the process of representation, the adult can make nonintrusive comments about what the child has observed or experienced about the subject being represented. These conversations need not be long but can help children access memories and analyze their own drawing to see what more they would like to add or change. When children are doing observational drawing, the teacher can share what she is observing about the item or scene.

Offer extensive material choices. When children are provided with many materials from which to choose, then they must think about how to make that choice and about the affordances, or capabilities, of different materials for different purposes. They need to think about what might work best in reaching their goal. Standard art materials, including a variety of paper, paint, and tools, should be available. In addition, there should be a convenient storage area for recycled materials, such as packing materials, recycled cardboard, and so on, for children to select from.

Provide a wealth of reference materials. Set aside a table or shelf where children can independently access books and artifacts that relate to the topic. Keep books and other material organized so children can easily find what they are looking for.

Help children organize their work. They need to be able to consult their photographs, their observational sketches, their favorite books, and photos. Amber put questions, webs, drawings, and photographs on a large bulletin board, which children were free to add to and to study. Children always knew they could find what they needed by going to the board. Children also enjoyed showing their board and explaining it to visitors. Kathy Steinheimer at the Valeska Hinton Center encourages children to use poster board to organize their drawings, photographs, and sketches. These can be maintained by the children. For example, in a project on the Movie Theater, there were posters on the film projector, the popcorn machine, the marquee, and the seats. These function as file folders for young children. Older children can actually use hanging file folders in milk crates that are conveniently accessible.

Encourage children to solve their own problems. Don't be too quick to jump in and solve children's representation problems. Children benefit from trying to work out problems on their own. When they discover that they can figure out their own ways to do things and are not dependent on adults, they feel empowered and competent. Self-esteem develops when children become confident in their own skills. Providing opportunities for children to solve their own problems also encourages the development of persistence. It is tempting for teachers to solve children's problems or to preplan so there is no opportunity for children to fail—to be successful at everything they do. There is danger in this philosophy as children can develop an unrealistic idea of how life's challenges are to be handled. To build resiliency in children, help them learn that they have talents and capabilities that they can use when needed. It is not, however, helpful for a teacher to withhold solutions to a problem when the child is clearly very frustrated. At this point, children benefit from alternative suggestions, joining with a buddy who can help, or a few well-placed comments that can focus thinking in a new direction.

Invite children to relook, rethink, and redo. Children need time to think and will often remember things that they forgot. Simply summarizing what children have shown or learned can encourage them to look again. Having thoughtful conversations with children about the content of their representations—for example, how a spider's leg has joints—can bring details to children that they hadn't noticed before. They will often think of ways they might then incorporate that into the representation. Children are also helped when teachers ask them to redo experiences, especially if a period of time has elapsed. The creation of Time 2, Time 3, or even Time 4 versions of a representation enables children to perfect what they are trying to accomplish at the same time that it enables children to build confidence in their abilities. Talking about what children have learned since the last drawing encourages the development of metacognition. Redoing doesn't have to always be the same media. Children can also use a variety of media in representation. For example, a child who creates a painting may be encouraged to use a three-dimensional media such as clay, still focusing on the same subject. Although these strategies take time, they contribute to the child's development of mind and brain capacity.

Provide time other than during project work for children to learn the strategies and methods for using a variety of media. Children will be able to use clay to represent what they are learning when they know how clay feels, how it can be shaped, and what it can and cannot do. It is probably not wise to teach young children a specific way to draw, such as finding shapes in an object. However, it is helpful for children to learn the basics of how to use a material, such as how much water to use in watercolor paint, how to wipe the brush on the edge of the glass, and how to put the brush on the paper.

It is helpful for young children to know how to knead, squeeze, and "pull out" clay. Marvin Bartel (2013), an art education specialist, makes a distinction between teaching young children techniques and teaching them "rituals." It is helpful for young children to learn the rituals of working with each media so they can be successful. There are many excellent books and resources that teachers can consult if they do not know these. Then children need to have time and experience just exploring the media, which means they need to be available in the classroom for use on a regular basis.

Keeping in mind the learning experiences of the children engaged in creating their own representations for their spider museum, let us return to the teacher-directed task of having all children in the class make paper-plate spiders. One of the dangers of learning experiences such as making a paper-plate spider is that messages, probably unintended, are communicated to children about their abilities. The task of making the paper-plate spider may have been difficult for one or more of these 4-year-old children, especially the accordion-folded paper legs. If a child was unable to do it and could not make his spider match the model, or if, even worse, the teacher "rescued the child" by doing it for him, then that child's disposition to represent and to create will be affected. The dispositions to use art materials to express his ideas and to think through and solve problems may have been damaged. The importance of Lilian Katz's dispositions theory was introduced in Chapter 2. A part of Katz's theory is the danger of damaging children's dispositions by what adults expect them to do. When a child cannot complete a representation on his own or when the child's work doesn't resemble the model, the child is less inclined to draw, create, and build in the future. If the representation based on a model is displayed next to those of more skilled peers, then the message about the child's ability is also communicated to parents and other adults. It is better to have children do their own individual representations, as in the Spider Project, and to have a teacher document the thinking and triumphs each child experienced in the process. Children's dispositions to be resourceful, curious, persistent, and creative are strengthened, and parents and others learn how their children can think and how they can support their children's thinking.

CHAPTER 7

Creating Provocations

A strategy for building mind and brain capacity in children is to create a compelling need for children to think deeply. When teachers consciously plan an activity or experience with the express purpose of creating deep thinking, it is called a *provocation*. In education, provocations are learning experiences designed to provoke thinking. Words used to describe provocations include *arouse, encourage, excite, fire up,* and *instigate*. Educators also use the term *higher-order thinking* as they discuss deep thinking. The application of knowledge through higher-order thinking skills is one of the purposes of the Common Core State Standards.

The most effective provocations have an emotional component that taps into the emotional energy that a child brings to a topic of interest. An example from Chapter 1 is Michelle's provocative question during the Seed Project when she asked the children what it would take to move the red pointer on a scale all the way to the end. Another example is the challenge of creating the Spider Museum described in Chapter 6.

Inserting provocations into project experiences is an effective way to deepen those experiences for children because they require action from the children (MBE Science Instructional Guideline 8). Provocations also enhance long-term memory of content because they support all three of the components of long-term memory (MBE Science Instructional Guideline 3). Children will be able to remember content that is emotionally important to them (value-laden memory) and that connects with what they already know (associative memory). A provocation can help a child see content knowledge and academic skills as something she needs to know (survival-value memory). A thoughtful provocation can motivate a child to learn and practice academic skills because he finds them to be useful in helping him respond to a challenge. A thoughtful provocation will often motivate a child to reach beyond her current level of functioning and try a new skill or to think at a higher level. Provocations also enable teachers to individualize learning experiences and involve children in the project at a greater variety of skill levels.

The term *provocation* appears often in descriptions of the preschools of Reggio Emilia (Katz & Cesarone, 1994). In those schools a provocation might consist of a special arrangement of materials or a change in the environment. The term is also used to describe a stimulating event or activity that gets children thinking about a topic (LeeKeenan & Nimmo, 1993). Provocations are used to begin or extend a project (Gandini, 1997).

There are probably as many ways for a creative teacher to provoke thought as there are languages of children. As teachers become more experienced in observing children closely and using what they observe to guide project work, they develop a repertoire of strategies for focusing children's thinking on the topic and connecting children to the project. Some teachers seem to easily think of provocations (on the fly during interaction during project work). There are many more teachers who appear to recognize a provocation when they see it in documentation of a learning experience or hear someone tell the story of a particularly thought-provoking event that happened in a classroom. There are, however, many teachers who have little idea of how they might go about creating a provocation within a project. When viewing a provocation that another teacher used, they wonder how the teacher thought of that or wonder if they could learn to do that. This is especially true of teachers whose training consisted mainly of teaching by following preplanned lessons or who have been teaching for a long period of time in a program that uses preplanned purchased curriculum plans.

There are many ways to provoke deeper thought in project work. The purpose of this chapter is to provide some ideas and inspiration from teachers in the field. When a name and classification are given to some of these ways of thinking about provocations, teachers can more easily discuss and share their thoughts and communicate with other teachers. A distinction is made between small-scale and large-scale provocations. Some provocations in project work result in those whole-class learning experiences described as orchestrated immersion in MBE Science (MBE Science Instructional Guideline 7). These are large-scale events such as the creation of the Seed Store or the Spider Museum. There are also many smaller provocations that occur throughout projects. At the end of the chapter are some strategies for teachers who want to add provocations to their project work or to improve the quality of provocations and thus increase the depth of thinking of their children.

SMALL-SCALE PROVOCATIONS

One way for a teacher to create more deep-thinking opportunities is to insert smaller, open-ended provocations throughout the project process. Small-scale provocations can even enhance unit or theme learning experiences during time periods when a project is not going on in a classroom. Small-scale provocations, as opposed to large-scale provocations, are less likely to have an overarching goal. Not all children respond to the provocation in the same way but in a variety of ways. These are often more open-ended.

Small-scale provocations support differentiation of instruction. They enable the teacher to integrate more options for individual children to connect with the project content and can be focused on the needs and interests of individual children. Small-scale provocations enhance the teacher's ability to observe, assess, and coach children at their individual level of understanding or skill, their zone of proximal development. Because these experiences are so open-ended, all children can find a comfortable entry point—one that taps into their neuronal network of prior experiences and what they know and can do. Each child is therefore more likely to have a learning experience that matches his development or skill level.

For example, a small-scale provocation might consist of taking children outside and asking them to collect one of each kind of leaf they can find. Inside the leaves can be placed on a table or a light screen for children to explore and use. One child might examine the leaves closely looking at the veins and stems. Another child might sort the leaves inventing her own criteria for sorting (e.g., size, shape, color variations, texture). Another child might trace or draw the leaves. Another might want to make a book of leaf shapes. Another child might ask for help to identify and learn the names of the plants from which the leaves were taken. In each of these examples, children are using higher-level thinking skills. All of the children are analyzing in some way. Some may form a hypothesis, and some may actually use the experience for creating something. As the teacher observes and interacts with the children, he can extend these provocations by varying how he frames his questions, describing and clarifying what children are thinking, reminding them of other similar experiences or concepts learned, or integrating new skills such as labeling or drawing. Small-scale provocations can be added to all phases of the project process.

Environmental Provocations

One way to create a small-scale provocation is to focus on the classroom environment. *Provocations within the environment* include the arrangement of the room and the placement of new opportunities within the room for different types of activities. One environmental change that can be especially provocative is the introduction of a new play environment. Teacher-made changes in the environment to provoke a related play episode usually happen in Phase I of the project approach during the time children are becoming familiar with the topic. For example, a teacher might change the family living area into a hospital by removing and replacing some of the furniture with other furniture such as a cot for a bed, a check-in area for children to do paperwork, and a doctor's area. This can be an effective provocation during this phase to build common background knowledge and vocabulary.

Creative dramatic play is, in many ways, the ultimate provocation for young children. Children must think of the role they might play, ways to use props, and how to communicate within that role. Children also have to constantly adjust their vision of the play scenario to adapt to that of other children. Involvement in a play episode connected to a project topic challenges children to think about what they must know to participate in the play; that is, what people in this situation do and think about. Because the play usually involves adults going about their business of living, children practice behaviors such as reading, writing, and using numbers to solve problems. The children see the value of these academic skills and the skills become important to them. In play episodes children learn and practice words related to the project topic such as *thermometer, blood pressure,* and *prescription.*

Although it may be tempting for the teacher to create a very rich, complex play environment for the children, it is more effective to keep this teacher-directed environmental provocation at a small scale and limit it to Phase I. The teacher can provide just enough to get the play going, to introduce vocabulary, and to provide an opportunity to assess children's understanding and skills related to the topic. This preserves the opportunity for a child-created play environment later in the project. During Phases II and III children can be challenged to expand their current play environment or to create a new large-scale environment. There is so much additional potential for mind and brain growth when children design their own play environments.

Another type of environmental provocation is moving furniture and creating new uses for areas. For example, a teacher might move easels to a new area, such as outside, placing them so they face something interesting to paint, such as fall leaves. Moving resources related to the project topic within the classroom (and outdoor) environment

is another way to provoke children's thinking. As mentioned in Chapter 6, for the Spider Project, Amber placed informational books on spiders in a basket in the outdoor play area along with some child-size lawn chairs. Having the books conveniently located where children are likely to encounter spiders encouraged children to immediately look for answers to their spontaneous questions. The chairs encouraged the children to sit and focus. The photos in the books enabled the children to analyze similarities and differences between the real spiders and the spiders in the books and to learn and apply the names of the parts of a spider to the specimens they found. Creating research areas for project work or designating a table or a shelf for project artifacts heightens children's curiosity about the topic, especially when the area includes books, photos, diagrams, and posters that children can access and use for independent research instead of being only accessible to the teacher. These environmental changes can empower children to find their own answers and take control of their own learning.

Materials Provocations

Another type of small-scale provocations is *provocations of materials.* Adding a thought-provoking material can be very simple, such as bringing an abandoned bird's nest into a classroom. Groups of items, such as different kinds of pine cones, can arouse children's curiosity. Sometimes arranging familiar materials or tools in a new way can provoke an exploration of their similarities and differences; for example, placing a variety of brushes on an art table with one color of paint helps the child focus on the brushes and how the shape and size create different effects on the paper. In a project on wheels, the teacher placed brushes of different widths with one color of paint (black) on the art table along with a tricycle wheel. Children became quite adept at choosing a brush that would make the best mark for the rubber section or for the spokes.

A small-scale provocation can provoke a whole project or determine the direction that a project might go. As described in Chapter 2, Lora Taylor placed a used camera in the housekeeping corner of her preschool classroom. As children began to play with the camera, she asked questions that provoked more play with the camera.

> The Camera Project started when a couple of children became really involved with a camera I had placed in the house corner area as a play prop to stimulate creative play. I thought the children might want to pretend to go places and take pictures. They took the camera outside of the play area and began running around the classroom saying, "Cheese." I questioned them:
>
> "What are you taking a picture of?"
>
> "What are you going to do with that camera?"
>
> (Helm & Katz, 2011, p. 77)

She added more cameras. Additional questions included, "How are you going to get the film out of there?" "How do you know that there are really pictures being taken?" (p. 77). The addition of the camera, the observation of the children's interest, followed by her thought-provoking questions, resulted in the Camera Project.

Placing materials in proximity to one another can result in a small-scale provocation. Creating an inviting display of materials paired with another interesting material will often provoke deeper work. For example, the introduction of a pumpkin on a table along with a tape measure invites children to combine these two materials. By placing a tape dispenser near the pumpkin on the table, the teacher enables children to come up with their own way to meet the anticipated challenge of getting the tape measure to stay in position for measuring. The addition of paper and pencil provides even more options in this mixed-age, 3- and 4-year-old classroom. Some children may simply have a sensory experience with the pumpkin, examining it and talking about it. Another child might pretend to measure by trying to wrap the measuring tape around the pumpkin as she has seen adults do. She might be joined by another child to work on the problem of getting the tape measure to stay in the center. As the teacher observes the children's interactions and conversations about the pumpkin and the materials, she can respond with provocative

questions appropriate for each child. A young 3-year-old may be fascinated with the shape and enjoy the feel of the pumpkin skin. The teacher may engage the child in a conversation and help him lift the pumpkin, turn it around, look at it from many sides. As he does so, she can be providing words so the 3-year-old can talk about what he is observing by using those words. The same teacher may ask the children who are struggling to get the tape measure to stay in position to articulate the problem and then challenge them for ways to solve it, hinting at the tape dispenser (see Figure 7.1). For the 4-year-old who is writing and knows many numbers, the teacher can challenge the child to record the results of this measuring. The teacher might even provoke some deep thinking by asking a child or small group of children, "What happens when we measure the pumpkin around the top, or around the bottom?" The open-ended nature of this experience enables the teacher to create individualized provocations as she interacts with the children as they interact with the material. Even more important, the openness of the material and the display with more than one option is a stand-alone provocation for the children to do what is comfortable but also be motivated to try something new. For example, the 3-year-old may also "write" numbers.

The provocation in Figure 7.1 may look familiar to teachers, who might recognize a variation on

Figure 7.1. Placement of materials together can become a small-scale provocation that children approach on a variety of levels.

this learning experience as a preplanned lesson in which the teacher brings in a pumpkin and demonstrates how to use the tape measure. For teachers learning how to create small-scale provocations in project work, I want to explain how this small-scale provocation is different from the preplanned lesson and what makes it a provocation.

- A provocation is open-ended, and children come to it because of what they find curious or interesting. In the preplanned lesson, the teacher demonstrates what to do. Children assume that is the task and may not consider other things they might do. They are less likely to approach the materials in another way or may shy away from the activity if they don't understand the purpose or think it might be too challenging.
- In a provocation, the child approaches the learning experience at an entry point that matches her prior knowledge and skills. In a preplanned lesson, the learning experience is set at the level of typical development for the age level of the children
- In a provocation, the teacher observes the children and shapes the experience to the zone of development for each child through her questions. She may introduce additional materials or share what she is seeing. In the preplanned lesson, the prior knowledge and level of development of children are assumed, and the task is designed for one level of development.
- A provocation is a learning experience designed to provoke children to think, to set a personal goal (such as measuring and recording), to work toward that goal, and to solve the problems encountered. In the preplanned lesson, the teacher does the thinking and planning, anticipating and avoiding problems in designing the experience. The teacher shows how to use cellophane tape to get the tape measure to stay in the center. The teacher is doing the problem solving and has taken this opportunity for problem solving away from the children.
- In a provocation, documentation and

assessment focus on each child's unique approach to the task. The teacher documents what the child can do and the child's individual knowledge, interest, and skills. In the preplanned lesson, the teacher observes and assists children in achieving the task and documents whether or not each child has achieved that specific task.

There are, of course, many times that children benefit from learning experiences that are teacher directed and teacher determined. There is nothing wrong with this preplanned lesson. However, if all of children's work is teacher planned and teacher determined, then children do not develop the capacity to do the higher-level thinking that they need to be successful. Project work is an opportunity for children to develop that higher-level thinking; however, if the learning experiences within the project are more like the preplanned lesson than the provocation described above, then the benefits of project work are limited. Making sure that children are having truly thought-provoking experiences within the project is an important part of facilitating project work. When a teacher becomes conscious and deliberate about incorporating provocations, even traditional early childhood experiences (such as measuring a pumpkin) can be reshaped to be thought provoking and result in significant intellectual growth. Adding an effective provocation can be as simple as a teacher stopping and thinking about an activity and how much thinking a child will actually do.

Language Provocations

Another way to challenge children to think is to provide *provocations of language and concepts*. One of the major tasks of children in the years before school and the early years of primary school is to learn words and what they mean. Vocabulary and word meaning are essential for good reading comprehension. One of the tasks of schools and centers in the early years is to expand the neuronal networks of children, especially those who come to the school environment with very few words. Increasing children's meaningful vocabulary requires that teachers provide experiences that enable words to move into long-term memory where they become accessible for later learning. All children benefit from deep thinking about words and their meanings, but provocations regarding language are especially important for children from low-literacy environments.

In the project approach, topics have been chosen because they are of great interest to children and connect to their world. Therefore, provocations that focus on project language and project concepts can be productive and effective ways to build vocabulary. Language provocations can be inserted easily into all phases of project work. Many teachers make a discussion of word meaning a standard part of all the projects they do. They create word-wall displays where important words are displayed with illustrations that clarify their meaning. Sometimes these are child made. Some teachers keep a list of words on a large sheet of paper, which they add to as new words are encountered during the project investigation. Other teachers create word cards, which are file cards with a project word and an illustration on each card. These are hooked together on rings and can be used by children to look up words when they are needed. First- and second-graders often make personal dictionaries of project words. Labeling artifacts and materials related to the project is helpful even if children are not yet readers because this helps adults interacting with children in the project to consistently use the same words so children are more likely to learn them. These are all good ways to focus children on the vocabulary of project work and make sure they have many opportunities to practice.

To provoke deeper and more meaningful thinking about project words, it works best to incorporate discussion, either whole-class or small-group, on language and terms. One way to do this is to bring up a word and ask children what they think it means. Definitions of words can, of course, be made up, and often children will come close to an official definition if they have had a lot of experience. However, the definition of a word is something that has already been decided, and understanding that words have common meanings is, in itself, a major cognitive understanding. Most often the provocation is to find who or what can provide a definition. This occurred in the Spider Project when Amber discovered that daddy longlegs were not spiders. Children were surprised by that and a discussion followed about what, then, was a spider. Word definitions can be fascinating to young children, and once they know a term, they will try to apply it. When children can identify the attributes of a word, they can then identify by comparing and contrasting what meets the requirements of the definition. For example, when they know the attributes of a spider, they can then sort out things that are and are not spiders. For example, ants and butterflies are not spiders. A language provocation would be for the teacher to bring in photos of butterflies, spiders, ants, and beetles, and during a small-group discussion, children can sort the photos into two groups—spiders and not spiders. Those children that master that cognitive task can then learn attributes of various types of spiders. This further delineation of a term into subcategories also occurred in the Spider Project as children first learned that some spiders make webs. In their investigation and observations, they discovered that there are different kinds of webs and that each of these kinds of webs has a different name (orb webs, tangle webs, sheet webs, and funnel webs). In this way they learned that words can enable them to tell others about what they found and also about what they were trying to create as they made their spider museum. They also develop confidence in their ability to learn words and use them. In the Spider Project, these 4-year-olds discovered that they could learn very large words such as "pedipalps" and "cephalothorax" and that it was fun to learn them and fun to use them. This type of language and concept provocation can be enormously empowering for children, especially for children who do not come from literacy-rich environments.

Small-scale provocations can be inserted in all phases of a project. A small-scale provocation late in Phase II or even early in Phase III can reenergize an investigation. For example, gathering photos from a field site visit and placing them on a poster board for children to discuss can motivate children to look at an aspect of the project topic that they haven't explored before. And thus a project investigation can become deeper and result in more learning.

LARGE-SCALE PROVOCATIONS

Large-scale provocations are those events or challenges that shape the direction of a whole project. These may serve as a catalyst for a deep investigation that lasts for months. Large-scale provocations can also emerge during the Phase II investigation and sometimes during Phase III as children decide how to share what they have learned. There are several ways that large-scale provocations frequently appear in deep project work. These provocations include large problems to be solved, challenges to represent thinking through art or media, or scientific experiments.

A Problem as a Provocation

Problems that young children encounter can be authentic and highly motivating. Children develop many executive function skills as they define goals and learn the value of persistence and hard work. When teachers keep their eyes open for big problems and challenges and recognize them as opportunities for children to become deeply involved in an authentic experience, great project work occurs. That is what happened in the Gong Stand Project in Dana Gorman's 4-year-old classroom at Community Cooperative Nursery School in Rowayton, Connecticut. The project began when Dana's class became intrigued with a set of classroom musical instruments and explored and discussed the instruments each day. Dana followed this interest by inviting some musicians into the classroom and arranging for the children to visit a few local bands to see, hear, and touch instruments that were not the same as those in the classroom set. During a field site visit to a local high school band class, the children became especially intrigued with a large free-standing gong. Back in their classroom, when drawing pictures of the trip, over two-thirds of the class drew a picture of the gong. Dana then remembered that there was a gong in a storage shed that had been given to the school to celebrate a former teacher's 10 years of service. There was, however, no gong stand. Dana found the gong and brought it to the classroom. The children were so excited when she pulled the gong out of the storage box. As it did not have a stand, Dana rested it on the carpet and held it upright with her hands. It was very heavy.

James: Wow! That is so big. I want to hit it!
Teacher: Here is the mallet, give it a try. [Child hits it.]
James: Hey, that doesn't sound right.
Alex: Let me try. You have to hit it harder. [Tries and is disappointed.]
Teacher: Does it sound like the one at the high school? [Children all say, no!] I wonder why this one sounds different.
Salman: Hey, it has holes in it, on the top.
Teacher: I see them; two on the top, and look, there is one on the bottom. Why do you think it has holes?
William: To hook it.
Teacher: What do you mean? Tell me more.
William: To hook it up
Teacher: Oh, it did come with this rope in the kit [shows rope].
William: Put the rope through the holes. And hold it.

Dana put the rope through the holes and held the gong up. The children hit it some more, and the sound was wonderful.

Teacher: This gong is very heavy. I cannot hold it here much longer. Let's look at the picture of the one we liked at the high school.
Cayden: It has a holder. This metal thing is holding the gong.
Teacher: Look at that. The gong is being held up by a stand.
James: We need a stand!
Teacher: I think we do. Hmmm, I wonder if we could try and build a stand for this gong. Would you like to try and do that?

A unanimous and excited yes resounded, and the Gong Stand Project began.

At first the children wanted the stand to be metal like the stand at the high school. Dana was concerned that she would not be able to find a metalworker or afford the materials and equipment needed to create this out of metal. Dana told them they could get a person who could help with a wooden one but not a metal one. So the children encountered their first constraint. The children started by creating various design ideas in the block center.

The children used pie plates, hole punchers, string, tape, and various shaped wooden blocks. The children tried out their ideas and came up with some very clever models (see Figure 7.2). During this time Dana consulted Joe, an adult with expertise in building who could help make their designs a reality. He helped Dana realize that with a very small budget and the fact that the gong stand would be kept outside, it needed to be built with pressure-treated 4 x 4s. That was the second constraint. She brought this information back to the children in class, and they went back to designing structures using only straight pieces of wood.

Dana also helped them measure how big the gong was. After finding the rulers to be too small, they used yardsticks and tape measures. The children took turns trying to hold the gong in the air and experienced how heavy it was. For some of the children it was as big as and maybe even heavier

than they were. The children and Dana talked a lot about how strong a stand would have to be to support such a heavy item. They also discussed how a gong moves when you strike it, so it had to be an open-ended structure.

Dana showed the children how to use the iPad to look up gong stands online. Some children sketched ideas from the photos online, others from their imagination, and others made sketches of their block gong stands (see Figure 7.3). Along the way they shared their ideas with one another.

As the children built larger block structures with straight pieces and then hit the pie plate gong, they started experiencing the structures falling. Dana initiated a class discussion on how to support the stand. The children went back to photos online and noticed that many of the structures had wider pieces on the bottom.

Noah: This keeps falling. The tape isn't working.
Teacher: I can see, when you hit the gong, the stand falls down. What could you do about that?
Noah: I can put blocks on the side to make it stronger. [Tries but it still falls.]
Teacher: Hmm, which way is it falling? [He points to the back.] Are there blocks there?
Noah: I can put more there. I'm going to make it taller, here and here [points to front and back].

Figure 7.2. The children designed their gong stands in the block area to try out ideas and plans.

Figure 7.3. Using clipboards to hold their papers, children recorded their thoughts about ways to make a gong stand.

Teacher: So you are going to put more blocks to support the sides. You are going to support it on each side of the tall pieces. [The teacher made sure to use the word *support* to help him learn that that is indeed what he was doing with the extra blocks.]

One day a child noticed the similarity of a gong stand to the tire swing outside. The children photographed the tire swing and talked about the angled pieces that supported the swing. Noah was familiar with the term *support* and could relate it back to his block creation. This design element became incorporated into their design.

After a couple of days focusing on the refined design, the children agreed on a design the class liked, a combination of a stand they had seen on line and the tire swing supports. They wrote up measurements and their plan and sent it home to Joe.

On the day of the build, it was drizzling and cold. When the children arrived on the playground,' Joe had the lumber out as well as all of the tools. He had the children's sketch and measurements hung up so the children could see their information and design utilized during the actual building. Joe kept referring back to the children's plan to know how long to measure each piece of wood for each cut. The children helped measure, carry lumber, sort hardware, drill holes, screw in the bolts, sand the pieces, and support the parts as they were attached to one another (see Figure 7.4). As they worked beside Joe, they learned new vocabulary words such as *drill bit, chuck key, right angle, circular saw, bolt, nut, screw, ratchet,* and many more.

After about an hour of building, the children took a break and went inside for snack. Small groups of children took turns going back outside. The children worked with Joe from 9:30 to 12:15. Then it was time to test their work. First Dana talked with the children about their predictions. Would the gong stand hold the gong? Dana placed it on the hook clips, and it worked! Testing the gong and hearing its glorious booming sound was an exciting reward for hard, sustained work! (See Figure 7. 5.)

Figure 7.4. Solving a problem together provides motivation for children and adults to connect and work as a team.

Dana describes the Gong Project this way:

The children were so proud of their accomplishment that day. They couldn't wait for their parents to pick them up from school so they could show them what they had done and let them try it. I received several emails that evening from parents telling me how their child had come home and explained the entire gong-stand building process to them and remembered so many of the terms and equipment used. The gong was dedicated in a lovely presentation ceremony and today it stands in our music area on the playground for all to enjoy.

This project is a wonderful example of a large-scale provocation. The need to solve a problem became the focus of the project. This project began as an exploration of musical instruments. The children were excited and interested in that broader topic, and Dana fully expected that they would continue to study instruments. However, as she watched the children respond at the high school

Figure 7.5. Having a functioning gong stand and banging the gong were natural rewards for the children's persistence and hard work.

band room and then saw that so many children focused their drawings on the gong, she realized that this instrument was exciting to them. It was then that she remembered the gong in the shed and went to find it, only to discover that there was no stand for it. This was a problem, as gongs have to have stands. Dana let the children discover the problem and then helped guide them through a very complex problem-solving experience.

Representation as a Provocation

Often a project can be extended when teachers continue to support children's interest even as a project is winding down. This is what happened in Dawn Johnson's 4-year-old, all-day prekindergarten program in Kids' World Day Care and Preschool in Centerville, Iowa. The children had become interested in fitness and working out when they noticed that their hearts would beat faster when they ran around the playground vigorously. A subsequent visit to the YMCA resulted in the children constructing a fitness center in their classroom, which they named Batman's Fitness Center.

The fitness center, however, was not the end of the project. The children wanted to know how exercise helped their bodies and began to ask what was inside their bodies. They were most interested in the brain, the heart, the stomach, and the lungs. The conversations and drawings focused on the body (see Figure 7.6). Dawn brought in nonfiction books for the children to look through, and they looked up these body parts on the Internet. One day, as Dawn shared photos she found online, the children noticed a picture of a skeleton displayed in a doctor's office. That's when they decided they wanted to make a human body. However, they didn't want "just a skeleton"; they wanted to construct all the organs. They had questions about the different organs. They looked through book after book examining pictures and asking questions of Dawn and her assistant. However, they did not seem to know how to begin making their human body model. One child asked, "How will the body stand up?" They had discussed how our bones give our bodies its form. "It needs bones!" exclaimed another child. When they answered that question, they were then able to begin building "Jessie."

Figure 7.6. Children's interest and understanding of how the stomach works can be seen in this drawing of a body.

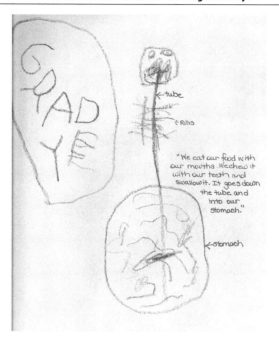

The children were very familiar with PVC pipes. There was a mini-chart stand and a tape holder in the classroom made of PVC pipe. One of the children said, "That stuff looks like bones. It's white, and it's hard." Dawn walked over to the chart stand and took it apart, showing them how the pieces fit together and how the pieces could be used to form the neck and shoulders. That's all that was needed. The children asked the teacher to buy more PVC pipe for the arms, legs, and so on. Dawn also made sure that the room environment supported their work. There were nonfiction books about the human body. The classroom already had a recycling bin in the art center; Dawn made sure that it was filled with materials that the children might want to use as they created their model of the human body (construction paper, tape, cellophane, contact paper, Ping-Pong balls, yarn, Q-tips, and so on.). Dawn added x-ray films to the light center so children could see what bones looked like. The children also had access to a small model of a skeleton in the science center.

At the beginning of January, the children began work on their human body model (see Figure 7.7). They formed research teams for the organs that most interested them: brain, heart, stomach, and lungs. The Brain Team was the first to meet. The teacher read books about the brain to the children. Bowen drew a picture of a brain and attempted to write the word. They learned that the brain is soft. Therefore, for their model they wanted to use a material that was soft as well. They decided to use cotton batting. A plastic container was used as the skull as it was hard—"hard like the ones in our heads." The children worked to glue the "brain" inside the "skull" (see Figure 7.8).

The Stomach Research Team was intrigued by how the food entered the stomach. The children listened to Dawn read books about the stomach to them. They learned that food goes down a tube in the neck called the esophagus. The children wanted to add an esophagus to the model. Triton located a paper towel tube in the recycling bin in the art center. They decided the tube would be used as the esophagus. They attached the tube with tape.

Ava said, "I remember the heart is a muscle. It is in our chest. It beats." Rilynn said, "It beats because it pumps blood in our body. It beats really fast when we exercise!" Dawn asked the children if they remembered how big the heart is. Josey held up a fist and said, "It's as big as my hand." Dawn confirmed Josey's comment and then asked the children what they thought they could use to make a heart. Ava said, "We could use paper. We have lots of paper in the art center. I could draw a picture of the heart on the paper with a crayon." Rilynn responded, "But there's blood in the heart. We can't get blood on the paper. That would make it disgusting!" Raegan agreed, "We can't put blood in the heart. Yuck!" Josey responded, "Let's see what Ms. Johnson has in the recycling bin." It contained a variety of items—craft sticks, balloons, bubble wrap, small cups, and so on. Rilynn said, "Let's use this!" She held up the bulb from a turkey baster which had broken. She said, "This squeezes like a heart!" The children wanted to put "blood" in the heart. Ava said, "Remember, Ms. Johnson used this with the tubes? She used red water in the tubes. Can we use some, too?" Josey asked, "How can we put the water in there?" Rilynn said, "We can use the funnel from the water center!" Raegan retrieved a funnel from the water center, and they put it in the turkey baster bulb. Ava carefully poured the water

Figure 7.7. Jessie, the human-body model created by preschoolers, required significant research and creative thinking.

Figure 7.8. The children wanted the brain to fill the head, be soft, and have lots of connections, so they chose cotton. The eyeballs had to be balls.

that the feather would be used. The children also added a paper nose, mouth, and ears to Jessie.

Most of the problem solving and higher-level thinking in "Making Jessie" centered around the materials to use for the model. The children were provided with a variety of materials, mostly from their recycling center. The children had a long and detailed discussion on how to make the feet for Jessie. Rilynn took charge of the process. She visited the recycling bin in the art center. A parent had donated some shoe inserts from a shoe factory. Rilynn selected two of the inserts. She said, "These are made like feet. I will use these!" She then selected a couple of pieces of cardboard from the bin. She carried the materials to the table. Rilynn said, "Jessie needs feet that are bigger than mine but smaller than yours, Ms. Johnson." Dawn asked her how she could measure the right size for the feet. Rilynn responded, "I can trace around your foot and make a smaller one." So, Rilynn traced around Dawn's foot on a sheet of paper and cut it out. She then used a crayon to trace the foot cutout onto the cardboard. That time, however, she cut *inside* the lines to make the foot smaller. Rilynn then wanted to tape the shoe inserts onto the cardboard foot to represent the toes. She said, "I can use tape to hold it." Rilynn had some difficulty in holding the inserts as she taped them to the cardboard. She said, "I need help with this." Triton volunteered to help. The two

into the bulb. Josey said, "We'd better put some tape on it, so the water doesn't come out."

The children wanted Jessie to look like a real person. Therefore, they decided that she needed a face. Several children worked on creating Jessie's facial features. The children chose Ping-Pong balls for the eyeballs and red yarn for the hair. Layla commented that the face needed eyebrows. She observed as Cadence and Samantha taped red yarn "hair" to the head. She ran over to the art center and selected a red feather. She brought it over and said, "We can cut this and make two eyebrows. See? It's the same color as the hair. My hair and eyebrows are the same color." The children agreed children worked together to cut the tape and hold down the inserts. Rilynn said, "The feet need to be the same size, because our feet are the same size."

Once the feet were made, the children had to figure out how to attach the feet to the body. Rilynn carried the feet to Jessie and slid the cardboard under Jessie's "legs." Dawn asked, "Is it going to stay on there, or do you need to do something to help keep her feet on there? What do you think?" Rilynn said, "I know! Tape!" Triton said, "Okay, tape. I'll get it." It truly was a team effort as Josey, Triton, Layla, Katie, and Ava lay on the floor and applied tape to attach the feet to the legs. Rilynn oversaw the project as she took ownership of the model's feet and wanted to make sure they were properly attached.

The making of Jessie was typical of complex experiences that occur in project work when children's interests are recognized and they are encouraged and supported in doing their own thinking and planning. These projects are the result of teachers recognizing the opportunity for deep, authentically engaging work that children can do. In the Gong Stand Project, Dana recognized that the lack of a stand was an authentic concern of the children. Dawn recognized that the children were extremely determined to build a human body. In the Seed Store Project that began this book, Michelle saw that children wanted to have their own Seed Store so they could play mixing and selling seeds. Opportunities for these large-scale enterprises emerge often in classrooms; however, in many cases, the opportunity is lost when the teacher is either unable or unwilling to nurture its growth. But when nurtured, these complex experiences seem to take on a life of their own. When a teacher integrates large- and small-scale provocations into the experience, they ignite discussions and debates, challenge children to solve problems, and provide a reason for children to create.

Variables as Provocations

Another way to provoke thought, especially about science topics, is to pay careful attention to children's questions and see if there is a question that can be "turned" into a scientific experiment to find the answer. During the preschool years children are beginning to develop the ability to do scientific thinking (Kuhn, 2002). Kuhn's definition of *scientific thinking* is "knowledge seeking . . . any instance of purposeful thinking that has the objective of enhancing the seeker's knowledge" (p. 372). Young children are always trying to make sense of their world, and in the process are developing theories, many of which are incorrect and are revised later as they gain more experience and evidence for and against their theories. Children are beginning to recognize situations in which two or more alternatives are possible, and it is not known which is true or correct. By ages 4 or 5, children recognize indeterminacy (that some things can be determined and some things can't be determined). This means they understand the difference between "Can tell" or "Can't tell" responses (Fay & Klahr, 1996). Preschoolers still tend to rely on their theories more than on evidence, but by the end of the preschool years they are able to begin using evidence to draw conclusions and find answers. At this time, it is important that children be able to respond to their own curiosity, pursue their own questions, and develop their own ideas. I have observed that preschoolers enjoy participating in "experiments" when these are included in project work.

Jelly (2001) suggests that a helpful teacher strategy is to examine children's questions and identify those questions that can be turned into a practical activity (experiment) in which children can use real materials or simulated real materials. She calls this teacher process a "variables scan" (p. 45). A *variable* is an element or feature that can vary or change. This means that it can be manipulated and experimented with to see how the change affects outcomes. There are a number of variable manipulations that can be understood and manipulated by preschool and early elementary children. Some variables that young children have experimented with in project work include what things are made of (e.g., toy bridge of play dough, wood, or paper), the length of time a process would take (e.g., whether to bake cupcakes for 2 minutes, 10 minutes, or 1 hour), and variations in what an animal will eat. Once a teacher recognizes that there is an opportunity for children to consider a variety of options, she can use questions to provoke the children's thinking. For example, in a project on bridges, the children may be interested in what bridges are made of. Indeed there is a variety of answers to this question, including wood, steel, concrete, rope, and so forth. Recognizing that there are many variables and that the children have an interest in that aspect of bridge building, she can bring the children's attention to the variety of answers possible. A question such as "If we are going to make a bridge in our classroom, what could you make it out of so it would be strong?" can be followed with "Can you think of some other things you could use to make your bridge?" and finally, "Which material do you think will make the bridge stronger and how could we test that?" By asking questions, the teacher has opened the children's eyes to possibilities and also helped them learn how they can purposefully organize their thinking, determine alternative solutions to problems, and draw conclusions.

For example, in the Gong Stand Project there were many variables for the children to consider when designing their gong stands: they could be circular or square; they could use wood or clay or metal. Sometimes, as in the Gong Stand Project, a question or a problem with a variety of solutions emerges quickly. Even very young children can "try out" alternatives on their own and observe the results, which is exactly what happened as the children designed their gong stands in the block area.

An opportunity to use variables as provocations happened in Christine Davidson's preschool classroom at the Center for Early Education and Care at the University of Massachusetts in Amherst. The children noticed a snake moving in the back of the flower garden along the edge of the building. One of the teachers was able to gently catch the snake so the children could examine it more closely. The children were interested in studying the snake further, so the next day Christine brought in a fish aquarium to make a temporary home for the snake. The children gathered leaves and grass to make the snake comfortable in the aquarium. The children talked about what the snake needed in its temporary home. When the children asked, "What do snakes eat?" rather than answer the question directly, Christine recognized that this was a question that could have many alternative answers. So she decided to let the children find out. She asked them what they thought. They suggested flowers, water to drink from rain, grass, salad, leaves, sticks, and worms. During morning meeting, Christine reviewed the list of all the snake-eating alternatives the children had made the day before. The children discussed ways to observe what types of food the snake would eat, and Christine helped them make a chart to try out their ideas. Another thought-provoking strategy is to encourage the children to predict what the answer might be, which is what Christine did with the children. After predicting what the snake might eat, the children and teachers went outside to collect the food items on the list.

The children tested their predictions by placing the food items in the aquarium with the snake. They watched and watched as the snake found the worm wiggling in the grass and then ate it whole! They continued to watch and watch, and the snake did not eat any of the other food items in the aquarium. They recorded their observations on their chart. The next day the children put another worm in the aquarium, and the snake quickly ate it up. The previous day's conclusion was confirmed. They concluded that snakes eat worms (see Figure 7.9).

Another example of young children's purposefully directed thinking occurred in the Chicken Project in Pam Scranton's preschool classroom, which was described in Chapter 6. During the project they had an incubator and hatched eggs. The eggs in the incubator had to be turned four times a day. The temperature and humidity levels in the incubator had to remain constant for the embryos to develop. The children realized that these were important tasks and that failing to do them would have dire consequences. A number of alternatives regarding how this could be accomplished were considered. The decision was to create a schedule, to have children create the schedule together so

Figure 7.9. Children recorded their findings of what the snake ate using this chart.

Snake Food?	Yes	No
Spider		✕
Worm	✕	
Stick		✕
Flowers		✕
Leaves		✕
Berries		✕

they wouldn't forget, and to write down when a child completed a task on the schedule. The children devised a plan for turning the eggs and also for checking the temperature and humidity levels each time (see Figure 7.10). Pam followed their directions and made a schedule chart on which the children conscientiously recorded completion of tasks. This is another example of children taking on serious jobs in project work.

STRATEGIES FOR CREATING PROVOCATIONS

There are many ways to provoke children's deep thinking in project work. Here are some strategies that teachers have found helpful:

1. Focus on how the topic connects to the children (their existing neuronal networks on this content topic). Begin conversation about the topic that authentically connects with children's lives. Get children to talk about the topic and share stories. Children who are kindergarten age and older can also draw and write about what they know.
2. Use the power of play as a provocation to connect children with the topic. Pretend play can build common background knowledge within the class and activate children's use of a beginning vocabulary about the topic.
3. In Phase II or III, challenge children to use the knowledge they have gained and their new vocabulary to create a complex child-designed play environment. Encourage children to play in it and to talk about their play.

Figure 7.10. The children quickly learned how to "read" the gauges of the incubator so they could check the temperature and humidity levels that were critical to the chick embryos' development.

4. Before using learning experiences that have been part of the classroom in the past, redesign them by changing the expected outcome, the materials available, or the instructions, so they are more open-ended and children can come to the experience at their own level of development.
5. Make changes in the environment (furniture, arrangement, the use of specific areas such as a block area or an outdoor play area) to integrate project content. Diversify the classroom environment so all children can find a place in the project work.
6. Make a list of materials that can be added to the classroom. Think about how more choices of some materials or less of another material can focus children on certain aspects of the project. Think about pairing materials and displaying materials in more thoughtful ways.
7. Review the teacher's anticipatory planning web. Make a list of specific areas in which

either small- or large-scale provocations might emerge or be teacher initiated. Note especially those opportunities for children to practice and achieve standards.

8. Review children's webs to identify any areas of misunderstanding. Then design a provocation that will enable children to discover or uncover information that will enable them to rethink those misunderstandings.

9. When reviewing children's questions, identify those to which children can find answers on their own. Encourage children to do their own research and investigation by asking them how they might find out.

10. Observe and listen closely as children work. Ask yourself, "How can I help this child think at a higher level?" Be thoroughly present and involved with the children as they work, rather than being an unengaged observer.

11. Help children build a repertoire of problem-solving approaches. Ask them what ideas they have. Remind them of what worked before. Provide alternatives when they become frustrated.

12. Watch for opportunities to integrate academic skills such as writing and use of numbers and data. Remind children when they can use a skill that they have previously learned. If they need to learn a new skill, offer to show them what they might do to continue their project work.

13. Watch for opportunities for a large-scale provocation to emerge, such as a big building project or a major question that must be solved. Don't be too quick to assume that a problem or plan is out of the range of what children of this age typically can do. Lift up the opportunity for the children, and let them know that this is something they could tackle with your help. Summarize children's thoughts and plans.

Provocations can become a highlight of a project both in engagement and in productivity for meeting curriculum goals and standards. As long as teachers remember that their purpose is not to provoke their own thinking but the thinking of the children, some wonderful learning experiences can result.

THE JOURNEY CONTINUES

We began our journey toward learning how to guide deep projects with new knowledge from Mind, Brain, and Education Science. As we end this phase of the journey, I would like to circle back to that foundation. In the Introduction, I defined deep project work, which can create mind and brain capacity. To review, deep project work

- Enables children to experience intellectual insight and depth of thinking.
- Is strongly connected to the children's world, involving them emotionally and sustaining intense interest.
- Is sensory rich with authentic artifacts and integration of complex knowledge.
- Provokes children to think deeply, to analyze, to synthesize new ideas, and to create meaningful artistic expressions, constructions, and other creations.
- Considers teachers as colearners.
- Motivates children to learn and practice academic skills.
- Supports curriculum goals and achievement of standards.
- Involves children in authentic explorations of the work that adults do.

Throughout this book I have shared excellent deep projects from many different settings. Strategies for enhancing project work have been presented, hopefully with enough detail that you will be encouraged to try them. In Appendix G, I provide a checklist review of the elements of deep project work, the MBE Science instructional guidelines, and the brain's executive functioning skills, so you can reflect on your own project work. Hopefully, you can work with a colleague or friend on this reflection process. Facilitating project work is so much easier when you share it with others.

Research, theories, methods, and strategies are helpful, and I have tried to provide you with some examples of each. But these don't capture what happens in deep project work. When deep project work occurs in classrooms, what I see is joy—joy in learning, joy in discovery, joy in using an intellectual mind (both children's and teachers'), joy in thinking and accomplishing meaningful work.

If we educators understand the message from neuroscience, we can't help but be hopeful. Children's intellectual destiny is not written at birth, nor is ours. We can build children's mind and brain capacity, and we can build our own. We can shape our classrooms, and what kind of teacher we want to be. We just have to have the courage to put away the workbooks, throw out our old lesson plans, forget about fancy bulletin boards and traditional units, and refocus on children. What are they thinking? What excites them? What do they want to play and do? What can we explore together? Go and do good work!

Categories of Information in MBE Science Applicable to Teaching

A Delphi expert panel assembled by Tokuhama-Espinosa (2008) developed a model of the new academic discipline of Mind, Brain, and Education Science. The panel reached consensus on 12 tenets that address individual learning, 21 principles of learning that are true for all learners, and 10 instructional guidelines. The group classified the information about the brain and learning identified in the literature review into four categories. These include (1) what is well-established, (2) what is probably so, (3) what is intelligent speculation, and (4) what is popular misconception or myth. In addition to agreement among the panel of experts, these concepts were also subjected to criteria from Best Evidence Encyclopedia and What Works Clearinghouse.

A. WHAT IS WELL-ESTABLISHED

A1. Human brains are as unique as faces; while the basic structure is the same, there are no two that are identical. While there are general patterns of organization in how different people learn and which brain areas are involved, each brain is unique and uniquely organized. (Tokuhama-Espinosa, 2008, p. 356)

A2. All brains are not equal in their ability to solve all problems. Context as well as ability influence learning. Context includes the learning environment, motivation for the topic of new learning, and prior knowledge. (p. 356)

A3. The brain is a complex, dynamic, and integrated system that is constantly changed by experience, though most of this change is only evident at a microscopic level. (p. 356)

A4. Human brains have a high degree of plasticity and develop throughout the life span, though there are major limits on this plasticity, and these limits increase with age. (p. 357)

A5. Connecting new information to prior knowledge facilitates learning. (p. 357)

B. WHAT IS PROBABLY SO

B1. Human brains seek and often quickly detect novelty, which is individually defined. (p. 165)

B2. Human brains seek patterns upon which they predict outcomes, and neural systems form responses to repeated patterns of activation (patterns being individually defined). (p. 162)

B3. Human learning is achieved through developmental processes, which follow a universal pattern for most skills, including academic skills shared across literate cultures, such as reading, writing, and math. (p. 371)

B4. The rehearsal of retrieval cues aids in declarative memory processes. (p. 281)

B5. The elaboration (overt teaching) of key concepts facilitates new learning. (p. 321)

B6. Declarative knowledge acquisition depends on both memory and attention. (p. 81)

B7. Nutrition impacts learning (good eating habits contribute to learning and poor eating habits detract from the brain's ability to maximize its learning potential). (p. 172)

B8. Water is "brain food." (p. 277)

B9. Sleep is important for declarative memory consolidation or the explicit learning that takes place in school (though other types of memories, such as emotional memories, can be achieved without sleep). Sleep deprivation also has a negative impact on memory. (p. 360)

B10. Stress impacts learning: "good" stress (eustress) heightens attention and helps learning, while "bad" stress detracts from learning potential. (p. 364)

B11. The human brain judges others' faces and tones of voices for threat levels in a rapid and often unconscious way, influencing the way information from these sources is perceived (i.e., valid, invalid, trustworthy, untrustworthy, and so on). (p. 360)

B12. Feedback and meaningful assessment are important to human learning, though the importance and role of feedback vary greatly across domains and processes. (p. 169)

B13. Self-regulation (monitoring oneself via executive functions) is an integral part of higher-order thinking skills. (p. 321)

B14. There are "sensitive periods" (not critical periods) in human brain development in which certain skills are learned with greater ease than at other times. (p. 177)

B15. Emotions are critical to decision making. (p. 357)

B16. Support (academic, moral, or otherwise) from others (often teachers, peers, or parents) is critical for optimal academic performance. (p. 168)

B17. When a learner actively constructs knowledge, the learner will be motivated and engaged in learning. (p. 159)

B18. The search for meaning is innate in human nature. (p. 159)

John Dewey's Vision of Project Work: How Close Am I?

John Dewey's Thoughts	How does this happen in projects in my classroom?
Aim of education is to enable individuals to continue their education—to *build the capacity for growth.*	
Nature of Young Child: • *Social Instinct*—conversation, personal intercourse, and communication to connect their experiences. • *Constructive Instinct*—the impulse to make things. • *Instinct to Investigate*—to find things out. • *Art Instinct*—the expressive impulse.	
Role of the Teacher: *Facilitate or guide* in the project process, a colearner, a member of the community of learners— still directs the activities through organization of materials, equipment, and experiences.	
Topic Selection: Provide *authentic explorations* related to the occupations of adults in a democratic society; authentic meaningful work. That is, topics should link to the real work of society (study, learn about the world, serve one another, create).	
Role of Experts and Field Site Visitors: Bring children into *contact with adults* who are doing adult work. Let children make their own observations of people—what they do, how they behave, what they are occupied with and what comes of it. Must be *action*—"go, movement, sense of use and operation."	
Authentic Artifacts: *"Real" things* should be part of the classroom, real objects and artifacts.	

Common Core State Standards and Project Work for English Language Arts in Kindergarten

A = Almost always happens in project approach in kindergarten
I = Can be integrated by teacher selection

Common Core Standard	A/I	What Happens in Project Work
READING STANDARDS FOR LITERATURE		
Key Ideas and Details		
• With prompting and support, ask and answer questions about key details in a text.	I	Listens to and reads *realistic fiction books or poetry* on project topic. Listens to and reads about authentic experiences of children and adults with the project topic, e.g. a book about going to the pumpkin farm in the pumpkin project.
• With prompting and support, retell familiar stories, including key details.	I	
• With prompting and support, identify characters, settings, and major events in a story.	I	Identifies from books what people do related to the project topic
Craft and Structure		
• Ask and answer questions about unknown words in a text.	A	Listens to and reads books and poems about the topic. When available, large books are used so children can see text. Learns to read project words (such as "turtle"), then find it in books. Listens to and reads *realistic fiction books* about the story and talks about the pictures and adventures and activities of people. Listens to and reads fantasy stories such as *The Very Hungry Caterpillar* <u>after children have completed their investigation</u> of real caterpillars. Compares and contrasts what happens in real events, for example, caterpillars and what real caterpillars eat as learned through their investigation and resources.
• Recognize common types of texts (e.g., storybooks, poems).	I	
• With prompting and support, name the author and illustrator of a story and define the role of each in telling the story.	I	
Integration of Knowledge and Ideas		
• With prompting and support, describe the relationship between illustrations and the story in which they appear (e.g., what moment in a story an illustration depicts).	I	Listens to and reads *realistic fiction books* about the topic and talks about the pictures and adventures and activities of people. Compares experiences related to the topic in the book and their field site experiences.
• With prompting and support, compare and contrast the adventures and experiences of characters in familiar stories.	I	
Range of Reading and Level of Complexity		
• Actively engage in group reading activities with purpose and understanding.	A	Participates in discussion about realistic fiction and what they learned about the topic from the book.
READING STANDARDS FOR INFORMATIONAL TEXTS		
Key Ideas and Details		
• With prompting and support, ask and answer questions about key details in a text.	A	Learns how to use informational materials and how to identify project words and main concepts related to the topic (e.g., the names of different seeds). Uses informational books, articles, and pamphlets or catalogs brought to the classroom for project work for research on project topic.
• With prompting and support, identify the main topic and retell key details of a text.	I	
• With prompting and support, describe the connection between two individuals, events, ideas, or pieces of information in a text.	I	
Craft and Structure		
• With prompting and support, ask and answer questions about unknown words in a text.	I	Teacher reads aloud informational books and shows how words related to the topic can be found and questions can be answered by using the book. Children become familiar with the structure of a book and how the author answers questions.
• Identify the front cover, back cover, and title page of a book.	I	
• Name the author and illustrator of a text and define the role of each in presenting the ideas or information in a text.	I	

Common Core Standard	A/I	What Happens in Project Work
Integration of Knowledge and Ideas		
• With prompting and support, describe the relationship between illustrations and the text in which they appear (e.g., what person, place, thing, or idea in the text an illustration depicts).	I	Uses informational books about the project topic. Compares illustrations to real artifacts in the classroom. Discusses why author chose to use an illustration or photo and what it shows. Compares different books about the project topic. Talks about differences in the books and how each might be helpful, for example, a plant dictionary versus a how-to garden book.
• With prompting and support, identify the reasons an author gives to support points in a text.	I	
• With prompting and support, identify basic similarities in and differences between two texts on the same topic (e.g., in illustrations, descriptions, or procedures).	I	
Range of Reading and Level of Text Complexity		
• Actively engage in group reading activities with purpose and understanding.	A	Listens to and reads books related to the topic with the purpose of finding answers to questions and deepening understanding of the topic. Listens to complex books about the topic and uses photos, drawings, and diagrams in texts for older children for research on the topic.
READING STANDARDS: FOUNDATIONAL SKILLS		
Print Concepts		
• Demonstrate understanding of the organization and basic features of print.	A	Participates in group reading of books and pamphlets about the topic. Teacher discusses print concepts. Reads big books, posters, and other authentic print artifacts related to the project. Class participates in dictating and reading emails to and from experts.
✓ Follow words from left to right, top to bottom, and page by page.	A	
✓ Recognize that spoken words are represented in written language by specific sequences of letters.	A	
✓ Understand that words are separated by spaces in print.	A	
✓ Recognize and name all upper- and lowercase letters of the alphabet.	I	
Phonological Awareness		
• Demonstrate understanding of spoken words, syllables, and sounds (phonemes).	I	Teacher uses project words as encountered in project research to teach phonological awareness, words, syllables, and sounds (e.g., "pizza").
✓ Recognize and produce rhyming words.	I	
✓ Count, pronounce, blend, and segment syllables in spoken words.	I	Children create and read Project Word List posted in the classroom, finding specific words as needed by using initial sounds.
✓ Blend and segment onsets and rhymes of single-syllable spoken words.	I	
✓ Isolate and pronounce the initial, medial vowel, and final sounds (phonemes) in three-phoneme (consonant-vowel-consonant, or CVC) words. (This does not include CVCs ending with /l/, /r/, or /x/.)	I	Teacher uses books, poems, catalogs, internet pages about the topic and demonstrates how awareness, words, syllables enable project words to be found and identified.
✓ Add or substitute individual sounds (phonemes) in simple, one-syllable words to make new words.	I	
Phonics and Word Recognition		
• Know and apply grade-level phonics and word analysis skills in decoding words.	I	Topic words are discussed as the teacher posts them on signs, labels, word walls, and other places. Adults help children with phonics and word recognition in pursuit of project goals.
✓ Demonstrate basic knowledge of one-to-one letter-sound correspondences by producing the primary sound or many of the most frequent sounds for each consonant.	I	
✓ Associate the long and short sounds with the common spellings (graphemes) for the five major vowels.	I	
✓ Read common high-frequency words by sight (e.g., the, of, to, you, she, my, is, are, do, does).	I	
✓ Distinguish between similarly spelled words by identifying the sounds of the letters that differ.	I	
Fluency		
• Read emergent-reader texts with purpose and understanding.	I	When available on the topic, emergent-reader texts are used to find information to answer questions, create representations, or prepare for presentations.

Common Core Standard	A/I	What Happens in Project Work
WRITING STANDARDS		
Text Types and Purposes		
• Use a combination of drawing, dictating, and writing to compose opinion pieces in which they tell a reader the topic or the name of the book they are writing about and state an opinion or preference about the topic or book (e.g., My favorite book is...).	I	Incorporates writing experiences as the need to write occurs. Incorporates project work and project words into journal writing, and other writing events. Students create their own labels for pictures and word walls. Children record answers to questions and interviews. Emergent-reader texts are read to find information to answer questions, to create representations, and to plan.
• Use a combination of drawing, dictating, and writing to compose informative/explanatory texts in which they name what they are writing about and supply some information about the topic.	A	
• Use a combination of drawing, dictating, and writing to narrate a single event or several loosely linked events, tell about the events in the order in which they occurred, and provide a reaction to what happened.	A	
Production and Distribution of Writing		
• With guidance and support from adults, respond to questions and suggestions from peers and add details to strengthen writing as needed.	I	Contributes to classroom and hallway displays on project topic, writes words or dictates narratives about the history of the project, a component of the project (such as a field site visit), or a description about what they learned about the project topic.
• With guidance and support from adults, explore a variety of digital tools to produce and publish writing, including in collaboration with peers.	I	Shares writing with work group and teacher making changes as needed. Participates in creation of PowerPoint presentations, electronic web page, or published book about the project.
Research to Build and Present Knowledge		
• Participate in shared research and writing projects (e.g., explore a number of books by a favorite author or express opinions about them).	A	Investigates the topic with others and writes responses. Generates, writes, asks questions of experts; finds answers through observation and investigation; gathers together conclusions and shares in Phase III of the project.
• With guidance and support from adults, recall information from experiences or gather information from provided sources to answer a question.	A	
SPEAKING AND LISTENING STANDARDS		
Comprehension and Collaboration		
• Participate in collaborative conversations with diverse partners about kindergarten topics and texts with peers and adults in small and larger groups.	A	Shares and discusses background knowledge about project topic, contributes to web of what is known. Has conversations with experts and field site staff. Talks about representation and sharing what was learned.
✓ Follow agreed-upon rules for discussions (e.g., listening to others and taking turns speaking about the topics and texts under discussion).	A	Participates in small- and large-group discussions on project work in all phases, participates in decisionmaking regarding how to investigate and how to share what was learned.
✓ Continue a conversation through multiple exchanges.	A	
• Confirm understanding of a text read aloud or information presented orally or through other media by asking and answering questions about key details and requesting clarification if something is not understood.	A	Participates in conversations day-to-day as project progress is discussed, plans are made, and experiences are debriefed. Generates questions for investigation with the class, asks individual questions of adults, expert visitors. Records answers and shares with class. Shares answers to investigation questions that were found in books and other resources.
• Ask and answer questions in order to seek help, get information, or clarify something that is not understood	A	Discusses with teachers and others what questions were answered and for which ones help is needed. Shares ideas for getting help. Explains answers to others and helps others understand concepts.
Presentation of Knowledge and Ideas		
• Describe familiar people, places, things, and events and, with prompting and support, provide additional detail.	A	Talks about prior experience with the topic in Phase I. Talks about what they saw and learned about on field site visits and with experts. Illustrates answers to questions of experts. Creates diagrams and thoughts. Adds to and does additional versions of drawings and other representations (Time 1 & Time 2). Describes what was learned on field site visits or from experts, explains ideas for solving problems or plans for representations.
• Add drawings or other visual displays to descriptions as desired to provide additional detail.	A	
• Speak audibly and express thoughts, feelings, and ideas clearly.	A	

Common Core Standard	A/I	What Happens in Project Work
LANGUAGE STANDARDS		
Conventions of Standard English		
• Demonstrate command of the conventions of standard English grammar and usage when writing or speaking.	A	Generates questions for experts and field site hosts. Works with peers to shape investigation.
✓ Print many upper- and lowercase letters.	A	Creates, models, drawings, and presentations of how things work and explains them.
✓ Use frequently occurring nouns and verbs.	I	
✓ Form regular plural nouns orally by adding /s/ or /es/ (e.g., dog, dogs; wish, wishes).	I	
✓ Understand and use question words (interrogatives) (e.g., who, what, where, when, why, how).	A	
✓ Use the most frequently occurring prepositions (e.g., to, from, in, out, on, off, for, of, by, with).	A	
✓ Produce and expand complete sentences in shared language activities.	A	
• Demonstrate command of the conventions of standard English capitalization, punctuation, and spelling when writing.	I	
✓ Capitalize the first word in a sentence and the pronoun I.	I	
✓ Recognize and name end punctuation.	I	
✓ Write a letter or letters for most consonant and short-vowel sounds (phonemes).	I	
✓ Spell simple words phonetically, drawing on knowledge of sound-letter relationships.	I	
Vocabulary Acquisition and Use		
• Determine or clarify the meaning of unknown and multiple-meaning words and phrases based on kindergarten reading and content.	A	Learns and uses project words, contributes to project word wall.
✓ Identify new meanings for familiar words and apply them accurately (e.g., knowing a duck is a bird and learning the verb *to duck*).	A	Sorts, classifies, and uses labels of artifacts related to the project that share common characteristics (e.g., the different seeds birds eat). Learns project words and how to use them. Defines new words and uses them correctly in conversations and play scenarios. Participates in conversations, interviews, surveys, and presentations using project words and phrases.
✓ Use the most frequently occurring inflections and affixes (e.g., -ed, -s, re-, un-, pre-, -ful, -less) as a clue to the meaning of an unknown word.	I	
• With guidance and support from adults, explore word relationships and nuances in word meanings.	I	
✓ Sort common objects into categories (e.g., shapes, foods) to gain a sense of the concepts the categories represent.	I	
✓ Demonstrate understanding of frequently occurring verbs and adjectives by relating them to their opposites (antonyms).	I	
✓ Identify real-life connections between words and their use.	I	
✓ Distinguish shades of meaning among verbs describing the same general action (e.g., walk, march, strut, prance) by acting out the meanings.	I	
• Use words and phrases acquired through conversations, reading and being read to, and responding to texts.	A	

Note: Standards are taken from *Common Core State Standards*, by National Governors Association Center for Best Practices & Council of Chief State School Officers, 2010. They are available online at www.corestandards.org.

Common Core State Standards and Project Work for Mathematics in Kindergarten

A = Almost always happens in project approach in kindergarten
I = Can be integrated by teacher selection

Common Core Standard	A/I	What Happens in Project Work
COUNTING AND CARDINALITY		
• Know number names and the count sequence.	A	Teacher identifies and obtains artifacts related to the topic that can be counted, compared, measured, classified, and grouped. Teacher also talks with experts about what objects they sort and classify in their work and asks to borrow some for the classroom, especially items of groups from 1 to 20. Students count and record items on field site visits, parts of things (e.g., tires or teeth, number of headers on a combine). Students compare numbers of things counted (e.g., cars versus trucks, kinds of seed)
• Count to tell the number of objects.	A	
• Compare numbers.	A	
OPERATIONS AND ALGEBRAIC THINKING		
• Understand addition as putting together and adding to, and understand subtraction as taking apart and taking from.	A	Teacher talks with experts about the addition and subtraction needs they might share with students. Teacher asks experts and field site hosts about the counting, adding, or subtracting they do. Children solve simple authentic problems related to topic. They use project objects or drawings of project objects to solve problems. (E.g., The veterinarian has five dogs in his hospital but only three dog bowls in the cages. How many dog bowls does he need to get out and put in cages?)
NUMBER AND OPERATIONS IN BASE TEN		
• Work with numbers 11–19 to gain foundations for place value.	I	Project artifacts are used for counting and recording. The teacher discusses the need for numbers beyond 10 and how to record.
MEASUREMENT AND DATA		
• Describe and compare measurable attributes.	A	Measure and compare two project objects that have a measurable attribute in common (e.g., which plant is the tallest? The tomatoes or the green beans? "Which plant has the most tomatoes that are ready to pick?) Classify project objects and count the number of objects in each category.
• Classify objects and count the number of objects in each category	A	
GEOMETRY		
• Identify and describe shapes.	I	Use shapes to describe artifacts, machinery parts, fruits, and any other object when applicable.
• Analyze, compare, create, and compose shapes.	I	Create drawings, models, and other representations in both two and three dimensions. Analyze the originals, talking about shapes and making a drawn plan before building.
MATHEMATICAL PRACTICES		
• Make sense of problems and persevere in solving them.	I	These mathematical practices are for all grade levels. Teachers look for opportunities in project work for students to solve authentic meaningful problems related to the topic that make sense and help students understand the value of mathematical thinking (e.g., how to create a slanted roof on a model barn using unit blocks). Teachers involve adults doing work related to the project to help create number problems for problem solving. Teachers encourage precision and accuracy in all project work, from counting and recording data, to creating realistic models or play environments. When students solve problems related to the project, the teacher remembers, then reminds them to think about how they thought through a similar problem, so they develop strategies.
• Reason abstractly and quantitatively.		
• Construct viable arguments and critique the reasoning of others.		
• Model with mathematics.		
• Use appropriate tools strategically.		
• Attend to precision.		
• Look for and make use of structure.		
• Look for and express regularity in repeated reasoning.		

Note: Standards are taken from *Common Core State Standards*, by National Governors Association Center for Best Practices & Council of Chief State School Officers, 2010. They are available online at www.corestandards.org.

Tying Together Curriculum Goals and Content Authentically

Use this sheet to practice authentically tying together a curriculum goal and a topic concept. By learning to think in this way you will be able to respond to children spontaneously in the process of project work. As with all new thinking skills, the more one thinks in this way, the faster and easier it becomes.

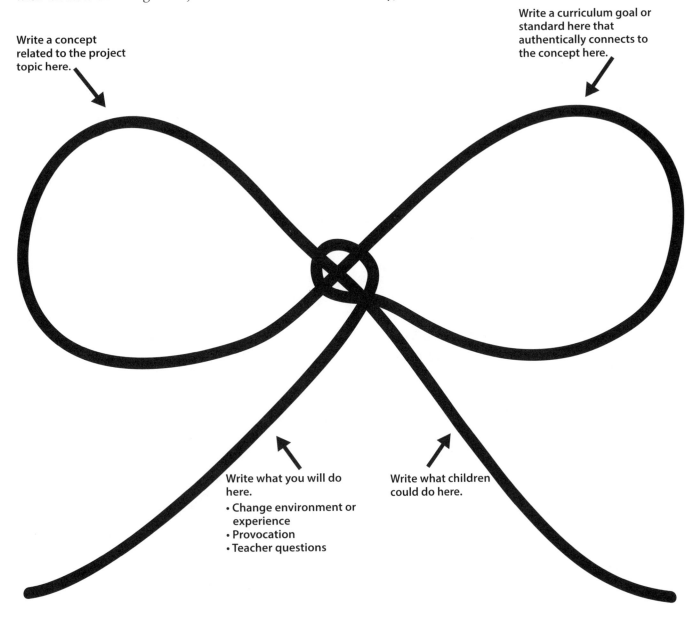

Write a concept related to the project topic here.

Write a curriculum goal or standard here that authentically connects to the concept here.

Write what you will do here.
- Change environment or experience
- Provocation
- Teacher questions

Write what children could do here.

Creating an Anticipatory Planning Web

To prepare: Select a worthwhile topic. Apply the rules of selection of topic.

Step One: Anticipate concepts that might be encountered in the project topic. Make an instructional web of *concepts about that topic*, placing the topic in the center. For example, for the topic of plants, concepts would include some plants grow from bulbs, bulbs come in different sizes (small, medium, large), bulbs store food. Plants need soil, water, sun to grow. Plants have parts, and so on.

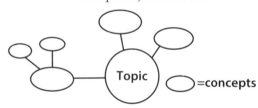

Step Two: Find authentic opportunities to integrate standards into the project. Examine the web, and add in curriculum—knowledge, skills, dispositions, or standards that are taught at your age/grade level—where they would naturally and authentically occur. For example, the natural place where a child would encounter measuring concepts would be "sizes of bulbs" or "heights of plants."

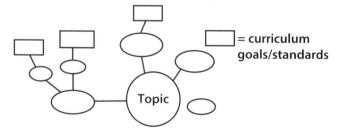

Step Three: Tie together standards and concepts about the topic. Look at the web you have created. Where the curriculum goal/standard and a concept come together, make a tie.

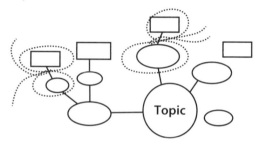

Step Four: Make a list of possible authentic activities to extend interest and tie goals/standards to content of interest. Use the tie to think about *authentic activities*. For example, an authentic use of numerals would be to find out the prices of seeds or the heights of plants or to record the number of rows of plants (as opposed to an unauthentic use of numerals such as teacher-made, construction-paper tulips with problems and sums written on them to be matched by the student). What can you do in the environment? What questions can you ask? What provocations will be helpful? Record those ideas in a list of possible project activities.

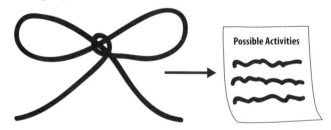

Step Five: Follow children's interest to narrow project topic. Begin some activities to introduce the topic (if not initiated by the students) and build background knowledge. Then follow students' lead and narrow the topic.

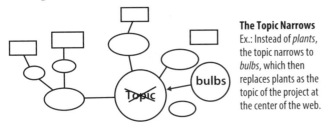

The Topic Narrows
Ex.: Instead of *plants*, the topic narrows to *bulbs*, which then replaces plants as the topic of the project at the center of the web.

Readjust techniques of instruction to match students' interest on this new narrower focus. Gather questions from the students. Investigate, represent, interview, and visit field sites. As student questions and comments emerge, keep revisiting the goals and standards that you want to accomplish and look for more ways to tie them to the content that the students find interesting.

For *standards* or *curriculum goals* not included in the project:

- choose to introduce in another mode *or*
- choose to cover at another time with another topic *or*
- do direct teaching if important but not emerging.

Reflecting on Project Work

Which Elements Typical of Deep Project Work Occurred in This Project?	Y/N or S (Some)	Observations
Topic was developmentally appropriate, curriculum connected, and worthwhile.		
Curiosity and engagement in topic was high.		
Focusing events occurred.		
Time for individual reflection on experiences with topic and opportunities to build background knowledge were included.		
Teacher assessed and recorded prior knowledge.		
Anticipatory planning of concept and curriculum integration was recorded in web or list.		
Children's questions drove investigation (including higher-level questions by children).		
Authentic artifacts were made available for investigation.		
Children had access to adult experts other than teachers.		
Ongoing documentation (photos of processes, not just products) was undertaken.		
Field site visits happened (may include within the building or nearby).		
Observational drawings and subsequent drawings were completed.		
Provocations were used by the teacher.		
Representations by children were true renderings of their concepts/ideas.		
Children and teacher had opportunities for metacognition.		
There was a summarization or presentation activity of what was learned.		
Families had opportunities to be involved.		

Reflect on your responses above, and write a short evaluation of the project.

Which Instructional Guidelines from MBE Science Occurred in this Project?	Y/N or S (Some)	Observations
1. **Learning Environment.** Intellectual conversations, clear vision of goals, student-centered activities.		
2. **Sense and Meaning.** Authentic experiences (natural contexts) connected to student; assessment of prior knowledge, culture considered.		
3. **Memory.** Activities support long term memory: *Associative*—links to past knowledge; *Emotionally* important—what the student gives importance to; *Survival value*—children know they need to know.		
4. **Attention Spans.** Engagement for short lengths of time alternating with time for reflection.		
5. **Social Nature of Learning.** Social interaction, discussions, working together.		
6. **Mind-Body Connection.** Attention to whole-child needs.		
7. **Orchestrated Immersion.** Differentiation of tasks, children come to project at different levels, a place for everyone.		
8. **Active Processes.** Limited passive listening, putting knowledge into action, includes higher-order thinking, skill development, building learning potential.		
9. **Metacognition.** Time to reflect upon learning, maximize memory consolidation.		
10. **Learning Throughout the Life Span.** Developmentally appropriate, age-related activities viewed as milestones and benchmarks, not for limiting what can be done or labeling children.		

Which Executive Function Skills Were Utilized in This Project?	Y/N or S (Some)	Observations
Hill: Goal setting and taking on challenges. Setting goals and focusing on learning what they want to know; self-directed learning. Recognizing that they want and need to know something.		
Skill. Actually makes connections, maintains focus, learns the skills necessary to do a task, stays engaged.		
Will. Follows through with goal, is persistent, tries to communicate with others, engaged in learning process.		
How well did this project build mind and brain capacity of children?		

Note: Concept of hill, skill, and will is taken from "'Hill, skill, and will': Executive function from a multiple-intelligences perspective," by S. Moran & H. Gardner, 2010, in L. Meltzer (Ed.), *Executive function in education: From theory to practice*.

References

Anderson, L. W., & Krathwohl, D. R. (Eds.). (2001). *A taxonomy for learning, teaching, and assessing: A revision of Bloom's taxonomy of educational objectives.* New York, NY: Longman.

Au, W. (2007). High-stakes testing and curricular control: A qualitative metasynthesis. *Eduational Researcher, 36*(5), 258–267.

Barell, J. (2007). *Problem-based learning: An inquiry approach.* Thousand Oaks, CA: Corwin Press.

Bartel, M. (2013). Teaching observation drawing to young children. Retrieved from www.bartelart.com/arted /coach2observe.html

Berk, L. E., Mann, T. D., & Ogan, A. T. (2006). Make-believe play: Wellspring for development of self-regulation. In D. G. Singer, R. M. Golinkoff, & K. Hirsh-Pasek (Eds.), *Play = learning: How play motivates and enhances children's cognitive and social-emotional growth* (pp. 74–100). London, England: Oxford University Press.

Berk, L. E., & Winsler, A. (1995). *Scaffolding children's learning: Vygotsky and early childhood education.* Washington, DC: National Association for the Education of Young Children.

Blair, C. (2002). School readiness: Integrating cognition and emotion in a neurobiological conceptualization of child functioning at school entry. *American Psychologist, 57*(2), 111–127.

Blair, C. (2003, July). *Self-regulation and school readiness.* (ERIC Digest No. EDO-PS-03-7). Retrieved from ecap .crc.illinois.edu/eecearchive/digests/2003/blair03.html

Blair, C. (2008). Executive functions and school readiness intervention: Impact, moderation, and mediation in the Head Start REDI program. *Developmental Psycopathology, 20*(3), 821–843.

Blair, C., & Razza, R. P. (2007). Relating effortful control, executive function, and false belief understanding to emerging math and literacy ability in kindergarten. *Child Development, 78*(2), 647–663.

Bloom, B. S., & Krathwohl, D. R. (1956). *Taxonomy of educational objectives: The classification of educational goals, by a committee of college and university examiners. Handbook 1: Cognitive domain.* New York, NY: Longman.

Bodrova, E. (2008). Make-believe play versus academic skills: A Vygotskian approach to today's dilemma of early childhood education. *European Early Childhood Education Research Journal, 16*(3), 357–369.

Bodrova, E., & Leong, D. (1996). *Tools of the mind: A Vygotskian approach to early childhood education.* New York, NY: Prentice Hall.

Boss, S., & Krauss, J. (2007). *Reinventing project-based learning: Your field guide to real-world projects in the digital age.* Washington, DC: International Society for Technology in Education.

Bowman, B. T., Donovan, M. S., & Burns, M. S. (Eds.). (2000). *Eager to learn: Educating our preschoolers.* Washington, DC: National Academy Press.

Catherwood, D. (2000). New views on the young brain: Offerings from developmental psychology to early childhood education. *Contemporary Issues in Early Childhood, 1*(1), 23–35.

Chouinard, M. M. (2007). Children's questions: A mechanism for cognitive development. *Monographs of the Society for Research in Child Development, 72*(1), i, v, vii–ix, 1–129.

Copple, C. (2012). *Growing minds: Building strong cognitive foundations in early childhood.* Washington, DC: National Association for the Education of Young Children.

Copple, C., & Bredekamp, S. (Eds.). (2009). *Developmentally appropriate practice in early childhood programs serving children from birth through age eight* (3rd ed.). Washington, DC: National Association for the Education of Young Children.

Dawson, G., & Fischer, K. W. (1994). *Human behavior and the developing brain.* New York, NY: Guilford Press.

Dewey, J. (1897). *My pedagogic creed.* New York, NY: E. L. Kellogg.

Dewey, J. (1915). *The school and society* (rev. ed.). Chicago, IL: University of Chicago Press.

Dewey, J. (1916). *Democracy and education: An introduction to the philosophy of education.* New York, NY: Macmillan.

Dewey, J. (1928). *The child and the curriculum.* Chicago, IL: University of Chicago Press.

Dewey, J. (1929). *My pedagogic creed.* Washington, DC: Progressive Education Association.

Dewey, J. (1933). *How we think, a restatement of the relation of reflective thinking to the educative process.* Boston, MA: D.C. Heath.

Diamond, A., & Lee, K. (2011). Interventions shown to aid executive function development in children 4–12 years old. *Science, 333*(6045), 959–964.

Dodge, D. T., Colker, L., & Heroman, C. (2002). *Creative curriculum for early childhood* (4th ed.). Washington, DC: Teaching Strategies.

Dombro, A. L., Jablon, J. R., & Stetson, C. (2011). *Powerful interactions: How to interact with children to extend their learning.* Washington, DC: National Association for the Education of Young Children.

Draganski, B., Gaser, C., Busch, V., Schuierer, G., Bogdahn, U., & May, A. (2004). Neuroplasticity: Changes in grey matter induced by training. *Nature, 427*(6972), 311–312.

Education. (n.d.). In *Dictionary.com.* Retrieved from the Dictionary.com website: dictionary.reference.com/browse/education

Edutopia. (2014). Project-based learning. Retrieved from www.edutopia.org/project-based-learning

Edwards, C., Gandini, L., & Forman, G. (Eds.). (1993). *The hundred languages of children: The Reggio Emilia approach to early childhood education.* Norwood, NJ: Ablex.

Edwards, C., Gandini, L., & Forman, G. (Eds.). (1998). *The hundred languages of children: The Reggio Emilia approach—advanced reflections.* Greenwich, CT: Ablex.

Epstein, A. S. (2007). *The intentional teacher: Choosing the best strategies for young children's learning.* Washington, DC: National Association for the Education of Young Children.

Fay, A., & Klahr, D. (1996). Knowing about guessing and guessing about knowing: Preschoolers' understanding of indeterminacy. *Child Dev, 67,* 689–716.

Fischer, K. W. (2009). Mind, brain, and education: Building a scientific groundwork for learning and teaching. *Mind, Brain, and Education, 3*(1), 3–16.

Fischer, K. W., Daniel, D. B., Immordino-Yang, M. H., Stern, E., Battro, A., & Klizumi, H. (Eds.). (2007). Why mind, brain, and education? Why now? *Mind, Brain, and Education, 1*(1), 1–2.

Fischer, K. W., & Immordino-Yang, M. (2008). Introduction: The fundamental importance of the brain and learning. In J.-B. E. Team (Ed.), *The Jossey-Bass reader on the brain and learning* (pp. 183–198). San Francisco, CA Jossey-Bass.

Flavell, J., Green, F., & Flavell, E. (1995). Young children's knowledge about thinking. *Monographs of the Society for Research in Child Development, 60*(1), i, iii, v–vi, 1–113.

Gandini, L. (1997). Foundations of the Reggio Emilia approach. In J. Hendrick (Ed.), *First steps toward teaching the Reggio way* (pp. 14–25). Upper Saddle River, NJ: Prentice-Hall.

Gardner, H. (1999). *Intelligence reframed: Multiple intelligences for the 21st century.* New York, NY: Basic Books.

Gardner, H. (2006). *The development and education of the mind: The selected works of Howard Gardner.* New York, NY: Routledge.

Gardner, H. (2008). *Five minds for the future.* Boston, MA: Harvard Business Press.

Gathercole, S. E., Pickering, S. J., & Stegmann, Z. (2004). Working memory skills and educational attainment: Evidence from national curriculum assessments at 7 and 14 years of age. *Applied Cognitive Psychology, 18,* 1–16.

Gillespie, L. G., & Seibel, N. (2006, July). Self-regulation: A cornerstone of early childhood development. *Beyond the Journal: Young Children on the Web.* Retrieved from journal.naeyc.org/btj/200607/Gillespie709BTJ.pdf

Glassman, M., & Whayley, K. (2000). Dynamic aims: The use of long-term projects in early childhood classrooms in light of Dewey's educational philosophy. *Early Childhood Research and Practice, 2*(1). Retrieved from ecrp.illinois.edu/v2n1/glassman.html

Grant, M. M. (2002). Getting a grip on project-based learning: Theory cases and recommendations. *Meridian: A Middle School Computer Technologies Journal, 5*(1). Retrieved from www.ncsu.edu/meridian/win2002/514/

Hardiman, M. M. (2012). *The brain-targeted teaching model for 21st-century schools.* Thousand Oaks, CA: Corwin Press.

Hardiman, M. M., & Denckla, M. B. (2010). The science of education: Informing teaching and learning through the brain sciences. In D. Gordon (Ed.), *Cerebrum 2010: Emerging ideas in brain science* (E-book). New York, NY: Dana Press.

Harlan, J. (1984). *Science experiences for the early childhood years.* Columbus, OH: Merrill.

Harms, T., Clifford, R. M., & Cryer, D. (1998). *Early childhood environment rating scale-revised.* New York, NY: Teachers College Press.

Helm, J. H. (2011). *Project approach implementation survey results.* Glenview, IL: Kohl Children's Museum.

Helm, J. H., Beneke, S., & Steinheimer, K. (2007). *Windows on learning: Documenting young children's work* (2nd ed.). New York, NY: Teachers College Press.

Helm, J. H., & Katz, L. G. (2011). *Young investigators: The project approach in the early years* (2nd ed.). New York, NY: Teachers College Press.

Holt, B.G. (1989). *Science with young children* (rev. ed.). Washington, DC: National Association for the Education of Young Children.

Illinois State Board of Education. (2013). *Illinois early learning and development standards.* Springfield, IL: Author.

Jelly, S. (2001). Helping children raise questions and answer them. In W. Harlen (Ed.), *Primary science: Taking the plunge* (pp. 36–47). Portsmouth, NH: Heinemann.

Jennings, J., & Rentner, D. S. (2006). Ten big effects of the No Child Left Behind Act on public schools. *Phi Delta Kappan, 88*(2), 110–112.

Jones, E., & J. Nimmo. (1994). *Emergent curriculum.* Washington, DC: NAEYC.

Katz, L. G. (1993). *Dispositions as educational goals.* ERIC Digest. Urbana, IL: ERIC Clearinghouse on Elementary and Early Childhood Education.

Katz, L. G. (2003). Building a good foundation. In J.H. Helm & S. Beneke (Eds.), *The power of projects: Meeting contemporary challenges in early childhood classrooms—strategies and solutions* (pp. 10–18). New York, NY: Teachers College Press.

Katz, L. G., & Cesarone, B. (1994). *Reflections on the Reggio Emilia approach. Perspectives from ERIC/EECE: A monograph series (No. 6).* Urbana, IL: ERIC Clearinghouse on Elementary and Early Childhood Education.

Katz, L. G., & Chard, S. C. (1989). *Engaging children's minds: the project approach.* Norwood, NJ: Ablex.

Katz, L. G., & Chard, S. C. (2000). *Engaging children's minds: The project approach* (2nd ed.). Stamford, CT: Ablex.

Kozulin, A. (2003). Psychological tools and mediated learning. In A. Kozulin, B. Gindes, V. S. Ageyev, & S. M. Miller (Eds.), *Vygotsky's educational theory in cultural context* (pp. 15–38). Cambridge, England: Cambridge University Press.

Kozulin, A., Gindes, B., Ageyev, V. S., & Miller, S, M, (2003). Introduction: Sociocultural theory and education: Students, teachers, and knowledge. In A. Kozulin, B. Gindes, V. S. Ageyev, & S. M. Miller (Eds.), *Vygotsky's educational theory in cultural context* (pp. 1–11). Cambridge, England: Cambridge University Press.

Kuhn, D. (2002). What is scientific thinking and how does it develop? In U. Goswami (Ed.), *Blackwell handbook of childhood cognitive development* (pp. 371–395). Malden, MA: Blackwell.

Kuo, Z. Y. (1976). *The dynamics of behavior development.* New York, NY: Plenum Press.

LeeKeenan, D., & Nimmo, J. (1993). Connections: Using the project approach with two and three year olds in a university laboratory school. In C. Edwards, L. Gandini, & G. Forman (Eds.), *The hundred languages of children: The Reggio Emilia approach to early childhood education* (pp. 251–268). Norwood, NJ: Ablex.

Linder, T. (2008). *Transdisciplinary play-based assessment* (2nd ed.). Baltimore, MD: Paul H. Brookes.

Markham, T., Larmer, J., & Ravitz, J. (2003). *Project based learning handbook: A guide to standards-focused project based learning for middle and high school teachers.* Novato, CA: Buck Institute for Education.

Marzano, R., & Kendall, J. S. (2006). *The new taxonomy of educational objectives.* Thousand Oaks, CA: Corwin Press.

Math and Science Partnership (MSP). (2010). What we know about deepening teachers' content kowledge: Engaging teachers with developing conceptual maps of mathematics/science content. Retrieved from the MSP Knowledge Management and Dissemination website:. www.mspkmd.net/index.php?page=12_2b

Moran, S., & Gardner, H. (2010). "Hill, skill, and will": Executive function from a multiple-intelligences perspective. In L. Meltzer (Ed.), *Executive function in education: from theory to practice* (pp. 19–38). New York, NY: Guilford Press.

Morton, B. A., & Dalton, B. (2007). *Changes in instructional hours in four subjects by public school teachers of grades 1 through 4* (Stats in Brief, NCES 2007-305). U.S. Department of Education, Institute of Education Sciences, National Center for Education Statistics.

National Governors Association Center for Best Practices & Council of Chief State School Officers. (2010). *Common Core State Standards.* Washington, DC: Authors.

New, R. (1990). Excellent early education: A city in Italy has it. *Young Children, 45*(6), 4–10.

NWO (Netherlands Organization for Scientific Research). (2010, May 17). Talking seriously with children is good for their language proficiency. *Science Daily.* Retrieved from www.sciencedaily.com /releases/2010/05/100512172529.htm

Perney, J. (2006). *Early Childhood Connections Project 2005–2006: Evaluation and assessment overview.* Glenview, IL: Kohl Children's Museum.

Pohl, M. (2000). *Learning to think—thinking to learn: Models and strategies to develop a classroom culture of thinking.* Cheltenham, Victoria, Australia: Hawker Brownlow Education.

Polman, J. L. (2000). *Designing project-based science: Connecting learners through guided inquiry.* New York, NY: Teachers College Press.

Rankin, B. (1992). Inviting children's creativity: A story of Reggio Emilia, Italy. *Child Care Information Exchange, 85,* 30–35.

Rice, M. (2012, February 17). Understanding the importance of self-regulation for preschoolers. *Innovations and Perspectives.* Retrieved from www.ttacnews.vcu.edu/2012/02/understanding-the-importance-of-self-regulation-for-preschoolers/

Rotherham, A. J., & Willingham, D. (2009). 21st century skills: The challenges ahead. *Educational Leadership, 67*(1), 16–21.

Shenk, D. (2010). *The genius in all of us: New insights into genetics, talent, and IQ.* New York, NY: Random House.

Smith, G. A., & Sobel, D. (2010). *Place- and community-based education in school.* New York, NY: Routlege.

Smith, L. (1997). Open education revisited: Promise and problems in American educational reform. *Teachers College Record, 99*(2), 371–415.

Sousa, D. A. (2010). *Mind, brain, and education: Neuroscience implications for the classroom.* Bloomington, IN: Solution Tree Press.

Sousa, D. A. (2011). *How the brain learns* (4th ed.). Thousand Oaks, CA: Corwin Press.

Squire, L. R., & Kandel, R. S. (2009). *Memory: From mind to molecules* (2nd ed.). Greenwood Village, CO: Roberts.

Sylwester, R. (2005). *How to explain the brain: An educator's handbook of brain terms and cognitive processes.* Thousand Oaks, CA: Corwin.

Tanner, L. N. (1997). *Dewey's laboratory school: Lessons for today.* New York, NY: Teachers College Press.

Thomas, J. W. (2000). *A review of research on project-based learning.* San Rafael, CA: Autodesk Foundation.

Tokuhama-Espinosa, T. (2010). *The new science of teaching and learning: Using the best of mind, brain, and education science in the classroom.* New York, NY: Teachers College Press.

Virginia Department of Education. (2010). *Science Standards of Learning for Virginia Public Schools.* Richmond, VA.

Vygotsky, L. (1966). Play and its role in the mental development of the child (C. Mulholland, trans.). Retrieved from www.all-about-psychology.com/support-files/play-and-its-role-in-the-mental-development-of-the-child.pdf (Original work published 1933)

Zull, J. E. (2002). *The art of changing the brain: Enriching teaching by exploring the biology of learning.* Sterling, VA: Stylus.

Zull, J. E. (2004). The art of changing the brain. *Educational leadership, 62*(1), 68–72.

Zull, J. E. (2011). *From brain to mind: Using neuroscience to guide change in education.* Sterling, VA: Stylus.

Index

About the Author

Judy Harris Helm, EdD, helps teachers of preschool through 3rd grade to integrate research into their curricula through her consulting company, Best Practices Inc. She is a national and international speaker and trainer on project work, engaged learning, documentation, and school design. Dr. Helm served as the educational planner for three early childhood centers and two birth–8th grade community schools. Included in the seven books she has authored or co-authored are *Young Investigators: The Project Approach in the Early Years*; *The Power of Projects*; *Teaching Your Child to Love Learning: A Guide to Projects at Home*; *Windows on Learning: Documenting Young Children's Work*; and *Teaching Parents to Do Projects at Home*.